AFTER EFFECTS

ON THE SPOT

TIME-SAVING TIPS & SHORTCUTS
FROM THE PROS

by **Richard Harrington,**
Rachel Max
& Marcus Geduld

DV EXPERT SERIES

Digital Video

CMP**Books**

San Francisco CA • New York NY • Lawrence KS

Published by CMP Books
an imprint of CMP Media LLC
Main office: 600 Harrison Street, San Francisco, CA 94107 USA
Tel: 415-947-6615; fax: 415-947-6015
Editorial office: 4601 West 6th St, Suite B, Lawrence, KS 66049 USA
www.cmpbooks.com
email: books@cmp.com

Designations used by companies to distinguish their products are often claimed as trademarks. In all instances where CMP is aware of a trademark claim, the product name appears in initial capital letters, in all capital letters, or in accordance with the vendor's capitalization preference. Readers should contact the appropriate companies for more complete information on trademarks and trademark registrations. All trademarks and registered trademarks in this book are the property of their respective holders.

The publisher does not offer any warranties and does not guarantee the accuracy, adequacy, or completeness of any information herein and is not responsible for any errors or omissions. The publisher assumes no liability for damages resulting from the use of the information in this book or for any infringement of the intellectual property rights of third parties that would result from the use of this information.

Cover design: Damien Castaneda

Distributed to the book trade in the U.S. by: **Distributed in Canada by:**
Publishers Group West   **Jaguar Book Group**
1700 Fourth Street   **100 Armstrong Avenue**
Berkeley, CA 94710   **Georgetown, Ontario M6K 3E7 Canada**
1-800-788-3123   **905-877-4483**

For individual orders and for information on special discounts for quantity orders, please contact:
CMP Books Distribution Center, 6600 Silacci Way, Gilroy, CA 95020
Tel: 1-800-500-6875 or 408-848-3854; Fax: 408-848-5784
email: cmp@rushorder.com; Web: www.cmpbooks.com

04 05 06 07 08   5 4 3 2 1

ISBN: 1-57820-239-6

CMP**Books**

Dedication

This book is dedicated to my wife, Meghan, and our first child.
—Richard Harrington

I'd like to dedicate this book to my family. Cheers for your support.
—Rachel Max

This book is dedicated to my lovely wife, Lisa, who makes me
feel blessed every day.
—Marcus Geduld

Contents

Introduction

Why did we write this book? We love After Effects. We use it ourselves almost every day to create motion graphics for our clients. We teach After Effects classes, give lectures, and consult one-on-one. And you know what makes us feel really good? When people learn a new trick or tip, smile, and say, "Wow!"

We still learn new tricks every day, and we still smile and say, "Wow!" We wanted to pass that excitement along. As much as we love this program, we can't teach everywhere, we can't answer the phone every night at 3 a.m. (our wives and roommates would kill us), and we can only get across so many tips in the time allotted to us at conferences.

So we wrote a book. The idea was to give the reader the cream off the top of the milk—just the good stuff. After Effects is a great program, with tons of features and shortcuts; the problem is separating the cream from the skim milk.

If you read every tech document on the web, perused every page of the manual, attended all of the Adobe training courses, and hung out with all the other AE uber-geeks, you'd have a bounty of knowledge (trust us, we have and we do). But you have a life, a job, and no time to dig to find those gems. If you're impatient, on a deadline, or just can't stand to look at another "Getting Started with After Effects" book, this book is for you.

All we ask is that you tell your friends about this book, and that when you win your first Oscar/Emmy (or make your first million dollars), you remember us—or, better yet, just smile and thank us at the next conference.

Who Is This Book For?

If you've worked with After Effects for a while and feel comfortable, you can get a lot out of this book. If you're a seasoned designer, we may help break you of some extremely slow habits and show you some really cool techniques. This book will help you move to a higher level.

If you've never opened the manual, read another AE book, or taken a training class—don't start here. You must learn to walk before you can run. If you're a "newbie," this book may leave you a bit overwhelmed. Buy it anyway, but read it after you've had some walking lessons.

With that said, don't try to read the book linearly. Shop for ideas, jump around a lot, and work your way through the chapters you need most. We've left extra space by the tips so you can jot down your own notes. If you're a mobile artist, this book should fit nicely in your bag. Hit a tough spot, and just pull the book out when the client leaves the room to check for a new idea or a troubleshooting tip. Have a few minutes to kill, read a tip. We bet you'll return to the application with some new ideas and new energy.

If you're looking for the little sidebars or tips in the margins, there aren't any. This whole book is filled with more than 400 tips. Get reading already—you've got a deadline to make.

Updates

Want to receive e-mail news updates for *After Effects On the Spot*? Send a blank e-mail to ae6ots@news.cmpbooks.com. We will do our best to keep you informed of software updates and enhancements, new tips, and other After Effects resources. Further, if you would like to contribute to the effort by reporting any errors or by posting your own tips, please contact the authors at www.rhedpixel.com, mgeduld@hotmail.com or books@rachelmax.com.

ON THE SPOT

Off to a Good Start:
Mastering AE's interface

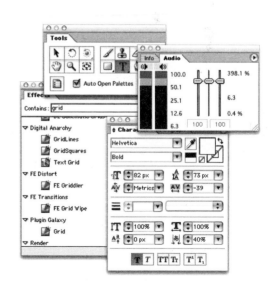

So you want to be fast? Concert pianists don't use a mouse to pick one note at a time from a menu; their hands flow across the keys. Don't think of After Effects as a tool; think of it as a creative extension.

Mastering the interface will keep you from stumbling in the dark, hitting the wrong keys, and making a lot of noise. You have to know what all your tools do, where to find them, and how to access their power instantly.

Over time, you'll gain confidence with all the controls. You want to be able to make the interface "disappear," which will allow you to reach "inside" the computer and create. Great designers know that the more brainpower they can put toward their graphics (not graphic system), the better the results.

Although learning an interface may not be as "fun" or "sexy" as a good effect, it's infinitely more important. Don't skimp on learning AE's interface–after all, you paid good money for a Baby Grand, so learn to play it well.

Change the Channel

When doing complex effects or color correction, it is often important to check the channel view of your footage. You can do this by clicking on the small strips of red, green, blue, or white (for the alpha) at the bottom of the comp window. These views can also be toggled from the keyboard. Press the following keys to switch between channel views:

To show the red channel	Option+1 (Alt+1)
To show the green channel	Option+2 (Alt+2)
To show the blue channel	Option+3 (Alt+3)
To show the alpha channel	Option+4 (Alt+4)

To toggle back, press the same keyboard shortcut again.

Take my Picture

Looking for a quick way to compare multiple frames within (or even between) your compositions? Instead of jumping around and waiting for AE to reload the frame, take a snapshot. After Effects supports a view of up to Four Snapshots.

❶ To Take a Snapshot, press Shift+F5, F6, F7, or F8. You can use any of these F keys (or even all of them) as a frame buffer.

❷ To view the Snapshot, just hold down F5, F6, F7, or F8 and it will load in the viewer as long as the key is depressed.

Get Your Toolbox Out

Need access to your tools? To change tools on the fly without clicking (or even seeing) the Tools Palette, try these shortcuts:

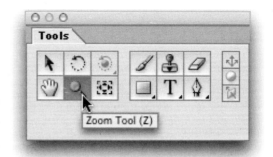

V	Selection Tool
W	Rotation Tool
C	Toggles between Orbit Camera, Track XY Camera and Track Z Camera Tools
H	Hand Tool
Z	Zoom Tool
Y	Pan Behind Tool (Also works as Trim)
Ctrl+B Cmd+B	Cycles between Brush, Clone Stamp, and Eraser Tools
Q	Cycles between Rectangular and Elliptical Mask Tool
Cmd+T Ctrl+T	Cycles between Horizontal and Vertical Type Tools
G	Cycles between Pen, Add Vertex, Delete Vertex and Convert Vertex Tools

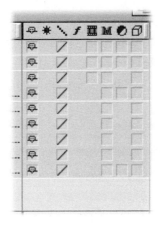

It's All Best in the End

Before rendering, it's important to ensure you are in best quality mode for each layer. On the other hand, draft mode is useful for speeding up previews. Looking for a quick way to flip a layer's quality switch from draft to full?

- Cmd+U (Ctrl+U) to switch selected layers to Best Quality.

- Cmd+Shift+U (Ctrl+Shift+U) to switch selected layers to Draft Quality.

Improve Your View

Is your comp window showing the controls you need? If not, bring the Comp View Options up. Go to the Comp Window and click on the triangular submenu or press Cmd+Option+U (Ctrl+Alt+U). Once there, you can modify several options including:

- Layer Controls visibility.

- Camera & Spotlight wire frames.

- Pixel Aspect Ratio correction.

A Working Canvas

By default, After Effects presents you with a black background in the comp window. While this is often useful, it may not work in all situations. Sometimes a contrasting background color may be needed when adjusting shadows or dark tones. Choose Composition>Background Color or press Cmd+Shift+B (Ctrl+Shift+B) to pick a new color. This color is temporary, and is not included in the render. It will be replaced with black when the comp is rendered.

Speeding up the Comp Window

Lowering the resolution of the Comp window can dramatically speed up previews. For example, switching from Full Resolution to Half Resolution speeds up previews four times (as it reduces both the width and height in half). In fact, previewing at half quality with the comp window set to 50 percent often provides a perfectly acceptable preview. To switch preview resolution quickly, use the following shortcuts.

For Full Resolution	Cmd+J (Ctrl+J)
For Half Resolution	Cmd+Shift+J (Ctrl+Shift+J)
For Quarter Resolution	Cmd+Option+Shift+J (Ctrl+Alt+Shift+J)

Welcome Back

When you launch After Effects, it can be a little lonely. You can quickly get back to the last project that you worked on. By default, After Effects tracks the last ten projects you've worked on. Simply go to File>Open Recent Projects, and pick. Or, if you want to go back to the last project you worked on, just press Cmd+Option+Shift+P (Ctrl+Alt+Shift+P).

No Canvas

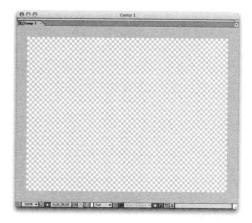

If you are a Photoshop user, you might be more comfortable working with a transparency grid instead of a colored background. In the submenu of the Composition window, choose Transparency Grid to set the comp window to transparent. When you render the file, After Effects will fill the transparency with black.

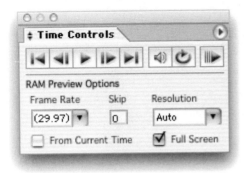

A Bigger Preview

Want to take your RAM previews full screen? By clicking the Full Screen box in the Time Controls Window, After Effects will do just that. When the RAM Preview is started, the screen goes black and the preview is loaded. Press the spacebar to start the preview mid-load. To exit, press the ESC key.

Clean Up Your Workspace

Have a few too many toolboxes open? Don't worry. You can quickly hide all floating toolboxes by pressing the Tab key. If you'd like to get rid of all floaters except the Tools palette, press Shift+Tab. This shortcut works in most other Adobe applications as well.

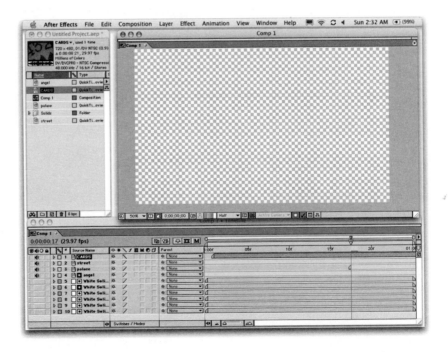

Opening Your Tool Chest

There are several floating palettes in After Effects, more than you'll usually want to deal with at once. To access the palettes, go to the Window menu or press the following shortcuts.

Cmd/Ctrl 1	Show/Hide Tools
Cmd/Ctrl 2	Show/Hide Info
Cmd/Ctrl 3	Show/Hide Time Panel
Cmd/Ctrl 4	Show/Hide Audio
Cmd/Ctrl 5	Show/Hide Effects and Presets Palette
Cmd/Ctrl 6	Show/Hide Character Palette
Cmd/Ctrl 7	Show/Hide Paragraph Palette
Cmd/Ctrl 8	Show/Hide Paint Palette
Cmd/Ctrl 9	Show/Hide Brush Tips Palette

Tools	⌘1
Info	⌘2
Time Controls	⌘3
Audio	⌘4
Effects & Presets	⌘5
Character	⌘6
Paragraph	⌘7
Paint	⌘8
Brush Tips	⌘9

A Sticky Drag

What we were thinking is that it would be pretty convenient to have dragged items snap to marks. By holding down the Shift key, your dragged item's in-point will snap to the current time indicator, markers, in- and out-points, and visible key frames. If you want to snap the out-point, hold down the Option (Alt) key.

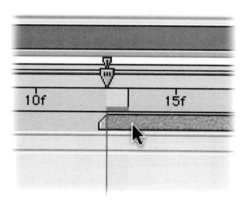

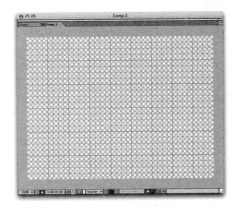

Grids

Grids can be useful when laying out your design freehand. To turn grids on, choose View>Grid or press Cmd+' [Single Quote] (Ctrl+'). Even more useful is the ability to turn on Snapping to the grid by pressing Cmd+Shift+' [Single Quote] (Ctrl+Shift+'). To adjust grid options, go to the preference menu and set frequency. (You have to have the Composition Window selected to use grids. Command+` toggles between the Composition Window and the Timeline. Command+Shift+` toggles between the Project Window and Comp Window.)

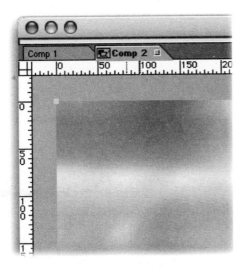

Using Rulers

Rulers are useful for checking the position of elements in your composition. Choose View>Show Rulers or Press Cmd+R (Ctrl+R) to bring them out. Once they're out, rulers can unlock a lot of useful features.

- You can adjust the rulers' center point by clicking in the upper left corner of the comp window. Click and drag to reposition the rulers.

- You can drag guides from the rulers for use in your composition.

- You can turn Snapping on for guides, by pressing Cmd+Shift+; [semicolon] (Ctrl+Shift+;).

- To toggle guide visibility, press Cmd+; [semicolon] (Ctrl+;).

- To lock guides in place, press Cmd+Option+Shift+; [semicolon] (Ctrl+Alt+Shift+;).

Visibility Powers

Need to toggle visibility on a layer? You can quickly turn a layer on or off by pressing

Cmd+Option+Shift+V (Ctrl+Alt+Shift+V). While that shortcut is pretty long, it is related to another. Pressing Cmd+Shift+V (Ctrl+Shift+V) will turn the visibility of all BUT the selected tracks off.

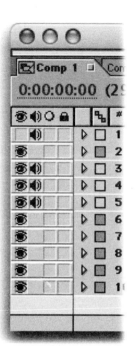

Power Scrub

Perhaps you've noticed how many input controls offer the ability to scrub, that is, to drag left and right on a property's name to adjust it numerically. If you're looking for greater control, however, try these two modifier keys when scrubbing.

Command (Control)	Scrub at a slower speed when adjusting values
Shift	Change scrubbing at a higher value

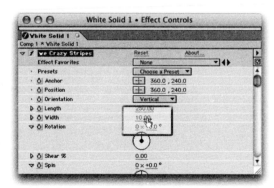

Clean Your Room

Looking for a fast way to get your windows back in shape? Maybe you've lost a window off-screen as well? Not a problem. To return to the default layout, simply choose Window>Workspace>One Comp view.

Build Your Own Room

You've configured your windows perfectly. Every palette and the time controls are exactly where you want them. The timeline has just enough room. Now save that window arrangement.

❶ Choose Window>Workspace> Save Workspace.

❷ Name the workspace and click OK.

❸ It now appears at the top of your Workspace list.

• After modifying a workspace, save it again with the identical name, and when prompted, choose Yes to overwrite the old workspace.

• Workspaces are saved in, and become part of your user settings when you quit After Effects.

• To delete a workspace choose Window>Workspace>Delete Workspace.

If You Don't Like Tabs

Are the tabs in the comp window or timeline annoying? Double click on the thin bar below the title bar, and the tabs will go away. This is also a good way to eke out a little more space when working on a laptop.

Give up Time, Get Back Space

When working on a small screen or laptop, the time controls are big. If you don't plan to change the preview options, click the up arrow next to the phrase 'Time Controls' to reclaim a good deal of screen space. When you need the extra controls back, click the down arrow or the Time Controls palette submenu.

If you decide to reclaim even more screen space, close the Time Controls palette entirely, and invoke a RAM preview by pressing 0 on the numeric keypad.

Get a Hand on Things

Need to pan around the comp window or timeline? Activate the hand tool by pressing the spacebar. This is a temporary switch. Adjust the viewed portion on the timeline or comp window, then release the spacebar.

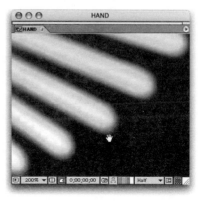

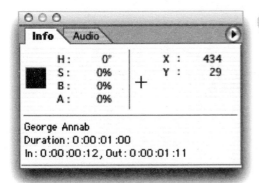

The Info-mation Age

The Info Palette is a hidden gem. To leave it open all the time, which we recommend, choose Window>Info or press Cmd+2 (Ctrl+2). Then, when you apply an effect, take a gander at it. Many effects print helpful information in the Info Palette. For instance, Particle Playground lists the current number of particles on the screen, and the 3D Channel effects list Z-depth information about any pixel you click. The only caveat is that you must bring up the Info Palette before applying the effect. If you bring it up after, you won't see the effect's info.

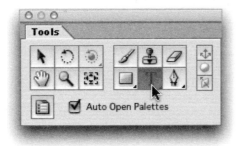

Where Did That Palette Come From?

Helper palettes should pop up when you click on the Type Tool, the Brush Tool, the Eraser Tool or the Clone Stamp Tool. When you click Type Tool, AE should automatically bring up the Character and Paragraph Palettes; when you click any of the brush tools (Brush, Eraser or Clone Stamp), AE bring up the Paint and Brush Tips palettes.

If you don't see palettes automatically popping up but want them to do so, select a tool and check the Auto Open Palettes option at the bottom of the Tools palette, which you'll see only when the Text, Brush, Eraser or Clone Stamp tool is selected).

If you'd rather not be surprised by pop-up palettes, uncheck the Auto Open Palettes option. You can manually summon the helper palettes by clicking the palette icon in the bottom-left corner of the Tools palette.

Mommy, I Lost My Effect

Those darn Effects categories! Where is Change Color, anyway? Adjust, Image Control? Stylize? Next time you're searching for an effect, don't click the Effect Menu and search through the categories. Instead, choose Window>Effects, or press Cmd+5 (Ctrl+5). A handy effects search engine will pop up.

In the text box at the top, start to type the name of the effect you want. If you type D, the window will list all effect names that contain the letter D. If you type Displace, the window will list Displacement Map, Turbulent Displace and Time Displacement. To apply an effect to the selected layer, double-click its name. Or, drag the effect from the Effect window and drop it on any layer in the Timeline or Comp Window.

A Smaller Preview

Wouldn't it be nice to focus only on what you care about? You can do just that in the AE world. Why preview the entire comp window when it is much faster to look only at the part of your composition that interests you. Here's how.

Enable the Region of Interest by clicking on the small icon next to the resolution menu in the comp window.

Drag out the area you'd like to see.

When starting a preview, only the highlighted area is seen.

To exit, click on the Region of Interest icon again.

Using Region of Interest has no impact on your rendered file.

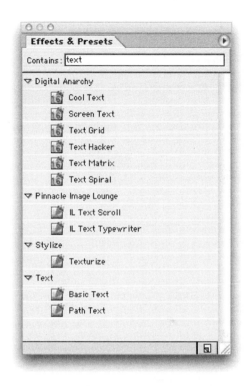

I Need Shades...

Most compositing Applications, such as Shake and Combustion, ship with the interface set to 50% gray. This makes it easier to make complex judgments about color and contrast. After Effects 6.5 now gives you the ability to adjust the brightness of windows and palette backgrounds.

❶ Choose Adobe After Effects>Preferences>User Interface Colors (Edit>Preferences>User Interface)

❷ Adjust the User Interface Brightness slider to adjust brightness.

A Longer Preview

Using a RAM preview in After Effects is great as it's a quick way to preview your work. Great that is until you run out of RAM! In After Effects 6, when you run out of RAM, AE must purge frames from the buffer.

After Effects 6.5 changes this though and helps speed up your workflow. Now when the RAM cache gets full, frames are cached to your hard drive. Don't worry though, you can set a cache limit and the cache is emptied when you quit AE.

To set up disk caching:

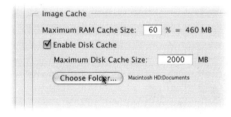

❶ Choose After Effects>Preferences>Memory & Cache (Edit>Preferences>Memory & Cache)

❷ Check the checkbox to Enable Disk Cache.

❸ The Choose Folder dialog box automatically opens and you need to specify where to write the cache. For best results place the frames on a local drive, but if possible, not the same drive as your source footage.

❹ Specify an amount for Maximum Disk Cache Size in megabytes (the default is 2000 MB.)

Send it Out

Mac users previously had the ability to preview their AE comps over Firewire or a video card. Now, with the release of AE 6.5, PC users can too! Plus Adobe has enhanced the ability of the preview all around. It is possible to preview the contents of a Layer, Footage, or Composition window on an external video monitor.

You can set Video Preview preferences by choosing After Effects>Preferences>Video Preview (Edit>Preferences>Video Preview). Choose one or more of the following interaction types.

- Previews: Both RAM preview and standard (spacebar) preview load on the external monitor. Choose Mirror on Computer Monitor to if you want to see the preview simultaneously on the computer screen and the external monitor, however mirroring reduces performance.

- Interactions: Interactive previews such as scrubbing and dragging in the Composition window on the external monitor. Interactive previews are always mirrored.

- Renders: Each frame is shown the external monitor during a render. All renders are also mirrored.

You can toggle video output by pressing forward slash "/" on the numeric keypad. This is a great way to turn this handy feature on and off.

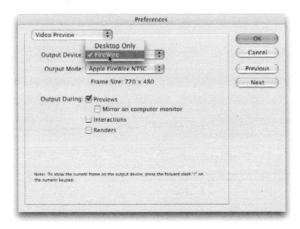

ON THE SPOT

CHAPTER 2

Animation Assistance:
Using Keyframe Assistants and Generators

Need to save time? Of course you do. Well, we can all use a little assistance.
Keyframe Assistants make it easier to get work done fast. Learn how to how to
fine-tune your animations and quickly achieve advanced effects. Whether it's to
generate keyframes or quickly align layers, these built-in tools can give you back
valuable time. Other powerful tools like parenting and Auto-Orientation allow
you to animate difficult relationships without getting keyframe intensive.

This chapter will help you save time by making several common tasks easier.
We'll also open up the door to some new tools and new uses that will help you
get more done.

It's Ease-y

Yummy. These keyframe assistants are like candy. They can definitely be overused but you can always tweak the default values.

Ease assistants allow you to quickly change keyframe interpolation method and velocity.

❶ Click on the keyframe where you'd like to apply ease.

❷ Choose Animation>Keyframe Assistant>and choose one of the following:

- Easy Ease–Gently move both into, and out of the keyframe.

- Easy Ease In–Slowly move into the keyframe, coming to a gradual stop.

- Easy Ease Out–Apply inertia to the movement out from the keyframe.

❸ Let's see this assistant in motion.

❹ Select a layer, and make two simple linear position keyframes.

❺ Do a RAM preview (hit Zero on the numeric keypad) to see the movement. Notice that the object moves at a constant rate.

❻ Select the end keyframe and choose Animation>Keyframe Assistant>Easy Ease In. Notice that the shape of the keyframe changes.

❼ Trigger RAM Preview again and notice that the layer's rate of movement slightly slows down as it reaches the second keyframe. The original rate of movement is slightly faster at the beginning point, then slows until finally stopping on the second keyframe. The spatial interpolation is still linear but the temporal interpolation is now Bezier. Notice that the motion path has a greater density of dots towards the second keyframe, meaning that velocity (or rate of movement) differs over time and velocity slows where there are more dots.

Convert Audio to Keyframes	
Convert Expression to Keyframes	
Easy Ease	F9
Easy Ease In	⇧F9
Easy Ease Out	⇧⌘F9
Exponential Scale	
RPF Camera Import	
Sequence Layers...	
Time-Reverse Keyframes	

And It Can Be Even Ease-ier

Want to reach your Ease assistants faster? Try these handy keyboard shortcuts.

Easy Ease	F9
Easy Ease In	Shift+F9
Easy Ease Out	Cmd+Shift+F9 (Ctrl+Shift+F9)

If you are running After Effects on Mac OS 10.3, be sure to change your default Exposé settings. If you don't, OS X will show all open windows.

Dance to the Music

This assistant is new to AE6. Previously you could use motion math or a third party plug-in like Trapcode's Sound Keys, but now, using audio amplitude to control other properties is native.

❶ Make sure you have at least one layer with audio.

❷ Set your work area to the length you want to generate keyframes.

❸ Choose Animation>Keyframe Assistant>Convert Audio to Keyframes.

❹ A new layer will be generated called Audio Amplitude.

❺ Select this layer and press U to reveal animating properties.

❻ After you reveal animated or modified properties, you'll see the assistant has created amplitude keyframes for the Left, Right, and Both Channels of the audio layer (or layers). Using a true stereo file will produce the best results as the left and right channels will vary. If you are getting the same amplitude levels for both left and right channels, you could disable them (by hitting the stopwatch) and just use Both Channels' keyframes.

❼ Now you can take a property of any layer or effect applied to that layer and use an expression to link the property to the audio amplitude. Amplitude tends to be low so you should add a multiplier at the end of your expression—like this Comp layer ("Audio Amplitude").effect("Right Channel")("Slider")*10.

Convert Audio to Keyframes
Convert Expression to Keyframes
Easy Ease   F9
Easy Ease In   ⇧F9
Easy Ease Out   ⇧⌘F9
Exponential Scale
RPF Camera Import
Sequence Layers...
Time-Reverse Keyframes

29

Convert Expression to Keyframes

You've written (or maybe just used) the perfect expression. Would you like more control over keyframe interpolation? Would you like to lock the expression in, AND speed up your render times? Then convert the expression to keyframes.

❶   Click on the expression you want to convert.

❷   Choose Animation>Keyframe Assistant>Convert Expression to Keyframes.

❸   Continue to modify keyframes as you see fit.

Line 'Em Up

The Sequence Layers' command is such a handy assistant to manage multiple layers. It's also a great way to get multiple footage items sequenced.

❶   Select the layers you want to sequence by selecting one, and then shift clicking or Cmd+clicking (Ctrl+clicking) on other layers to select them. The first layer you selected remains in its initial time position and the other layers will move to new positions in the timeline, depending on the order in which you selected them.

❷   Choose Animation>Keyframe Assistant>Sequence Layers.

Line 'Em Up and Fade 'Em Out

The Sequence Layers command also gives you the ability to dissolve between shots. Perform the Sequence Layers command as previously described. In the dialog box you have a few choices on overlapping the layers.

- You can select whether the layers overlap, and if so, how long they overlap.

- You can also choose to have the layers cut to another or dissolve between layers by adjusting the transition setting.

- Dissolve Front Layer when you want to dissolve between full-screen opaque items such as video or film footage.

- Cross Dissolve Front and Back Layers works well for items that have transparent areas (such as text or logos). This option causes both layers to fade and will show the background layer through.

Stop Motion in AE

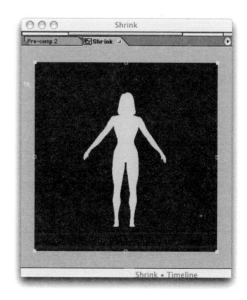

You can make a nice stop motion animation with sequence layers and an Illustrator file.

In Illustrator create a drawing in a layer

❶ Duplicate the layer, and modify it moving lines or segments.

❷ Repeat step one or more times ending up with a file where every layer contains a progression.

❸ Name your layers with numbers.

❹ In AE, go to File>Import>File and import that file as Composition Cropped Layers.

❺ Open the composition, select all the layers, go to 2 seconds in the timeline, and press Option+] (Alt+]) to trim the layers.

❻ Choose Animation>Animation Assistants> Sequence Layers.

❼ Press Cmd+K (Ctrl+K) to access Composition Settings and change the duration of your comp to at east 40 seconds RAM Preview.

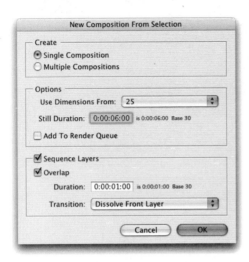

Gather 'Round for the Slideshow

The Sequence Layers command is useful for creating a slideshow from a series of stills.

❶ Select all of the stills you'd like to sequence.

❷ Drag the stills on the new comp icon in the bottom of the project window.

❸ Choose single composition.

❹ Specify which dimensions if the files differ.

❺ Select the duration for the stills here.

❻ Decide if you want to sequence the layers and if they should overlap. Use the Dissolve Front Layer option if you'd like to fade between shots.

❼ Click OK.

True Camera Scale (Pro)

Have you ever animated a scale from say 100 percent to 0 percent and have it look a bit off when you preview the animation? The human eye will pick up that the object appears to scale more quickly at the end of the scale. Mathematically it's taking the same amount of time to scale from 100 percent to 50 percent as it is to scale from 50 percent to 0 percent. Perceptually though, your eyes see more change occurring in the last half of the scale.

If you are using the Pro version of After Effects, take advantage of the Exponential Scale keyframe assistant.

❶ To fix this shift click on your two scale keyframes to select them.

❷ Go to Animation>Keyframe Assistant> Exponential Scale. This assistant will take a while to generate the new keyframes. This keyframe assistant speeds up the time spent on small degrees of change and elongates the time where more change is occurring creating an exponential curve.

It's a logarithm!

A Switch in Time

At any point you can select a range of keyframes and reverse their order. You can also select and reverse keyframes across multiple layers and properties.

❶ Select a range of keyframes by shift+clicking or lassoing around a range of keyframes.

❶ Choose Animation>Keyframe Assistant>Time-Reverse Keyframes.

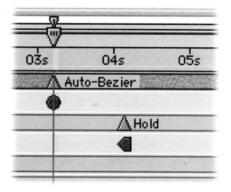

Keyframe Interpolation

The fundamental premise of After Effects is change over space and time. You effect change by applying keyframes. How those keyframes relate to each other is the basis of any animation. By default, After Effects is set to use linear keyframes, so there's a constant rate of change between keyframes. But a few simple shortcuts can quickly change keyframe types.

• Cmd+Click (Ctrl+Click) on a linear keyframe to change it to an Auto Bezier Keyframe. The keyframe will go from diamond shape to a circle and the motion will be slightly smoother. The timing or your animation is the same but the rate at which your object is moving has been slightly altered.

• Option+Cmd+H (Alt+Ctrl+H) to change any keyframe into a Hold Keyframe. Hold keyframes will hold a property value until another value is reached in the timeline.

• If you want to check what kind of keyframe you are dealing with, or if you want to switch which kind of keyframe to use launch the Keyframe Interpolation dialog box. To adjust keyframes manually choose Animation>Keyframe Interpolation or press Option+Cmd+K (Alt+Ctrl+K) to view your temporal and spatial interpolation.

Broken Keyframes

When adjusting the Bezier handles on a keyframe, it is possible that you can "break" your handles. If you want them to join again, try the following:

- Go to your interpolation dialog box. Context click on the keyframe for the floating menu, and change your Bezier Keyframe to a Continuous Bezier Keyframe.

- Option Double Click on the Keyframe for the Keyframe Velocity Box and check the Continuous Bezier Box.

- Bezier Keyframes have different incoming and outgoing velocities (broken handles) while Continuous Bezier Keyframes have the same incoming and outgoing velocities (joined handles).

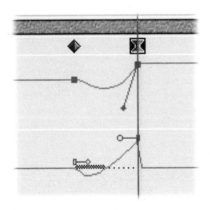

Graph It

The best way to understand what's going with your keyframes is to click the triangle next to the keyframes you've set. This will open up the Speed (or Velocity) Graph.

- Position and Anchor Point keyframes are spatial and will show the speed graph.

- Keyframes for Opacity, Rotation, or Scale, will show both a velocity graph (to show the rate of change) and a value graph (to show you degree of change).

- When you select a keyframe, you'll see blue handles, sort of like the Bezier handles on a motion path, which you can drag around.

- Dragging these handles up increases speed or velocity.

- Dragging these handles down decreases speed or velocity.

Keyframe Velocity

When you use the Ease Assistants After Effects is applying a 33.3 percent ease in the original velocity to the velocities of a keyframe. To see the numeric Keyframe velocity Option+Double Click on a keyframe, or press Shift+Cmd+K (Shift+Ctrl+K). You can modify incoming and outgoing influence and speed in this palette. You want precision? You've got it.

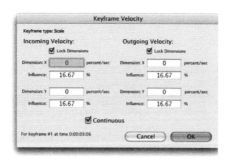

Draw Your Animation with Motion Sketch

Motion Sketch records the position of a layer and the speed at which you draw. It's great for when you want a layer to have an organic feel to it, or if you want your layer to follow a path that would be difficult to draw with the pen tool.

❶ Make sure your composition window is at 100 percent or higher magnification.

❷ Set your work area to the time you want to sketch for.

❸ Select the layer you want to animate, then go to Window>Motion Sketch. Although you can use your mouse to draw the path, Motion Sketch works best with a graphics tablet and pen. For snappier response, choose to show a wireframe of the layer. You may need to show the background for references your draw.

The capture speed is quite important. If you set the capture to 100 percent and your work area is 4 seconds, you will have 4 seconds to draw your path. If your capture rate is 50 percent you will only have 2 seconds in which to draw, but if your capture is 200 percent, you will have eight seconds to draw your path. Whatever capture rate you choose, your path will still play back realtime in four seconds.

You'll find, as you use Motion Sketch, that it is hard to draw a path in realtime, and you may choose to capture above 100 percent.

If you have an audio layer that you are trying to sync movement with, make sure your audio button is turned on in your Time Controls Window to hear it as you capture.

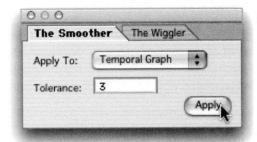

Smooth Operator

Continuing the tradition of goofy names for cool tools, we introduce the Smoother (What's next? The Jiggler and Tumbler?) The Smoother is used quite often in conjunction with Motion Sketch as sketching creates a lot of keyframes. You can also use it to reduce other generated keyframes from the Wiggler or Third Party Assistants.

❶ On the layer you just motion sketched, click the position property name to select all of the position keyframes.

❷ Go to Window>The Smoother. In this case you'll be smoothing the spatial path but the smoother can also be used on temporal keyframes like Opacity or Rotation.

❸ The tolerance defines how great (in pixels) the smoothed keyframes can vary from the original path. The higher the tolerance, the smoother the path. You may want to repeat the smoothing multiple times at a low value until the desired result is achieved.

Everything in Its Right Place

You could spend time eyeballing position but why when you can use the Align & Distribute Palette? You need least two layers to align and you need at least three layers to distribute.

❶ Select the layers and choose Window>Align & Distribute.

❷ Choose the icon representing the type of alignment or distribution you want.

• If you are aligning to a side move one of your files to the position you want and then select all and align to the right (or left, or whatever) because the alignment option aligns selected layers to the object that most closely represents the new alignment.

• A distribution option evenly spaces layers between the topmost and bottommost layers or furthest left and right justified layers. Locked layers won't be affected by alignment. It is best to work with layers of the same sizes since layer distribution is based on anchor points, which are usually in the center of the layer.

Motion Tracking (Pro)

You can track the motion of an object in a layer and then use the tracking keyframes generated to control the position of another object. The Tracker in AE6 is faster and stronger than ever before.

❶ Select your motion source layer, and choose Window>Tracker Controls. Select Track Motion. This will open the layer in the layer window and give you a tracking region. You need to find an area to track (high contrast, circles) such as with stabilization.

❷ Name your tracker in the Options Bar, and click OK. Once back in the Tracker Palette, hit the play button to analyze the track for the length of the comp. Scroll through the timeline to preview the analysis. If you find your tracker drifting, you can try resizing or moving the regions, and re-analyzing from that time. Nudge the regions, frame by frame, using the arrow keys.

❸ Try changing the Options. Track Luminance if your footage is high contrast or track Saturation if it is colorful. If you can't get good results going forward then start your track at the end of the footage and work backwards. When you are happy with your data, hit Apply. Go back into the Composition window, and do a RAM Preview to proof your track. Try using The Smoother to improve a track.

Tracker Attachments (Pro)

If you are unsure what layer you want to attach the tracking data to, or want to apply the data at a later time, choose Raw from the Tracking Type menu bar. The tracking data is stored in the motion source layer, where later on, you can use expressions to link a target layer.

If you have a layer in your composition that you want to attach to your tracking data, the tracker will default to using Transform as the Tracking Type. Transform tracks position and/or rotation with one-track point for position or two for rotation. Choose the layer you want to apply the data to in the Edit Target bar.

Tracking Tough Footage (Pro)

If your tracking gives you less than satisfactory results, give some of these options a try. While they'll take longer to process, you may get better results.

- You may want to track position and rotation, which will give you two tracking regions positioned diagonally. If the footage is interlaced, try tracking fields. If the shot has a lot of movement, try going to the final frame and tracking in reverse.

Try modifying the options by clicking the Options Button above the play button in the tracker controls palette. In AE 6.0, you need to click Options again near the tracker plug-in selector.

- In AE 6.5, the tracker window is simplified and you only need to click Options once.

- You can choose to track the RGB, Luminance, or Saturation Channels of a region.

- Try enhancing your footage by temporarily blurring or sharpening it. (The blur or sharpen is only for tracking and not actually applied to the layer).

- You can track using subpixel positioning where the tracker analyzes position between pixels, and you can tell After Effects to guess at the closest position with the Extrapolate Motion if Confidence is Below _%. The extrapolate option is handy for when your tracking feature becomes temporarily hidden.

Following Tracks: 2D Auto Orientation

As an object moves along its path, you have two choices. Either the object maintains its orientation, or the object rotates to follow the path. Think of this animation as similar to a roller coaster car on its track.

1. Select a layer for which you have already created position keyframes.

2. Choose Layer>Transform>Auto Orient or press Cmd+Option+O (Ctrl+Alt+O).

3. Choose Orient Along Path, and to deactivate it choose Off.

4. You will find this incredibly useful when you are animating insects, unidentified flying objects, bobsleds, or any other object that needs to follow a curved path.

Look at Me: 3D Auto Orientation

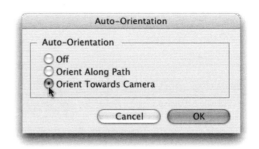

The best thing about Auto Orienting 3D layers is that you can orient them toward a camera. After Effects is not a true 3D program and layers in 3D space are flat. When you are animating a camera, move through layers in 3D space, select your layers, and choose Layer > Transform > Auto Orient or press Cmd+Option+O (Ctrl+Alt+O). Choose Orient Towards Camera to have your layers turn as the camera moves through them. This gives the illusion that the layers have some dimension.

Stay on Targets: Multipoint Motion Tracking (Pro)

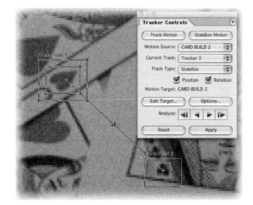

You can track more than a single point in a footage layer. If you wanted to replace a billboard, sign, or doorway in a clip you would use one of After Effect's multi-point trackers. These options are grayed out unless you have another layer in the composition to apply the data to.

- Parallel Corner Pinning, which is actually three-point tracking, is used to track things that stay parallel to the shot where you do not need to track perspective. If you have a perfect zoom into a window you would use Parallel Corner Pinning, for example.

- Perspective Corner Pinning is four-point tracking, and is used to simulate the distortion that occurs with perspective. This type of corner pinning is perfect for billboards, book covers, or any sort of four-cornered object with perspective skew.

- With both types of multi-point tracking the attach points mark the placement of the corner points. You can place the feature and search regions away from the attach points over areas with better contrast variations than there may be on whatever you are trying to cover up.

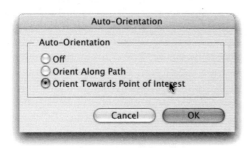

Faithfully Yours

When animating cameras, you may want to Auto Orient the Cameras to their Point Of Interest. This way, as the camera moves in space, its focus never wanders.

❶ Select a camera.

❷ Choose Layer>Transform>Auto Orient or press Cmd+Option+O (Ctrl+Alt+O).

❸ Choose Orient Towards Point of Interest, and to deactivate it, choose Off.

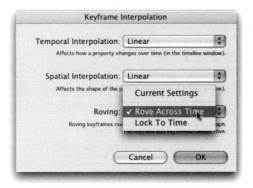

Roving Keyframes

After animating the position of a layer, you may decide that you want your rate of movement to be constant. You could fiddle with the speed graph by moving your keyframes closer together, or further apart to produce a flat velocity line, but why do that when there is a much easier method?

Roving keyframes, which are only available for spatial properties, were designed to do just this. Select all the keyframes you want to rove, and do one of the following:

• Go to Animation>Keyframe Interpolation, or press Cmd+Option+K (Ctrl+Alt+K) and, from the roving keyframe menu bar, choose Rove Across time. Notice your keyframes become auto Bezier except for the first and last.

• Alternately, open up the Speed Graph. and click on one of the boxes under any keyframe. Notice how the speed becomes a flat line indicating that it is constant. The keyframe shape has also changed to auto Bezier except for the first and last keyframes.

The first and last keyframes of the spatial property can never rove as they determine the intermediary keyframes' speed and time. This is great because when you want animation to occur over a shorter or longer time, just select the first or last keyframe and drag it closer to a linear keyframe to speed up the animation, or further away to elongate it. Notice how all your roving keyframes maintain the same constant speed.

Follow Me: Auto-trace

New to After Effects 6 is the Auto-trace option. You can convert the alpha, luminance, red, green, or blue channels of a layer to one or more masks. Once you have a mask, you can apply any mask-based effects.

Auto Trace is work-area sensitive so adjust your timeline accordingly. Instead of dragging the work area tabs, hit B to begin the workspace, and N to end it.

❶ Select your layer and choose Layer>Auto-trace to bring up the options box.

❷ For a less detailed trace, increase your pixel tolerance; for more detail, decrease tolerance. More detail means more time.

❸ Threshold is used to determine where to draw the mask, and is really intended only for layers without an alpha. Values over the percentage you enter are mapped to white, and made opaque. Values under the threshold are mapped to black, and are made transparent.

❹ You may find it useful to blur the image a few pixels before tracing. This will generate a mask with fewer points.

A Better Trace

If you'd like better results with the new Auto-trace command, take these extra steps before running the command.

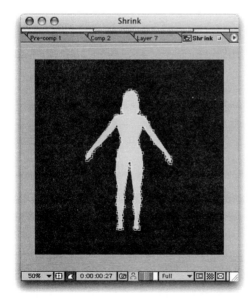

- If you are trying to trace a part of a layer, first mask out the areas you do not intend to trace. This will increase tracing speed and avoid unwanted masks.

- If you are using a channel to trace your masks, you may want to apply an effect, which increases the contrast of that channel like levels, channel mixer, or brightness/contrast.

Healthy Parent/Child Relationships

There was once a time in AE where you had to precompose and/or nest layers to group them but no longer! A parent layer assigns its transformations (all except opacity) to its child layer. The child is still independent of the parent though, and can have its own animations applied.

Think of it like your right arm (or left, if you prefer). Your fingers can wiggle on their own, yet they are parented to your hand. If the hand moves, the fingers move. Likewise, the hand is parented to the arm, if it were to swing outward, the hand (and fingers) would follow. And lastly, the arm is parented to your body. Where the body goes, the arm goes, and hence the hand, and likewise the fingers. One parent can control many layers but a child can only have one parent.

- If you don't see a Parent Column in the timeline, contextual click on the top of any column and choose Columns>Parent.

- Use the Pickwhip to drag and select, or manually choose a parent by clicking on None.

- If you are assigning a parent to many layers, select multiple layers and select a parent for one of them. The parenting will be applied to all selected layers.

- Parenting can not be animated. If you want to stop parenting at any time, you need to split the layer, and assign None as a parent to the split.

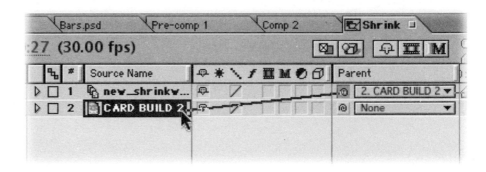

Come to Me: Parenting Using Null Objects

There are times when you will need to group layers, and you don't necessarily have a parent layer in mind. This is particularly true when working with 3D layers, and you want them to follow an object.

❶ Go to Layer>New >Null Object. Nulls are invisible but have all the transform properties of a regular layer.

❷ Select all of the layers you want to parent by shift clicking to select a range or Cmd+click (Ctrl+click) to select noncontiguous layers.

❸ In the parent column, choose Null1 or use the pickwhip.

❹ Now you can set keyframes on one layer to control a group of layers. This is especially great when you want several layers to rotate around a point in space.

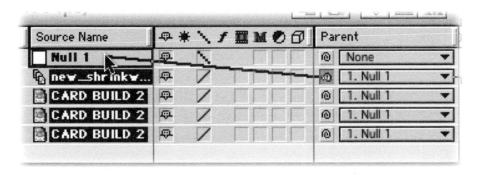

Here Kiddy-Kiddy

Wouldn't it be nice to be able to quickly grab a layer and all its children (sort of a digital minivan)? This way you could move their stacking order or flip a single 3D switch. Well in AE 6.5 you can! Simply contextual click on a parent layer and choose Select Children. Instant family reunion time.

Save Everything I

After Effects 6.0 allowed you to save filter combos as Effect Favorites. This was helpful, but didn't cover all the needs. But hey it wouldn't be an upgrade if there weren't changes for the better.

After Effects 6.5 introduces the concept of animation presets which allow you to save and reuse just about any animation.

Animation presets can contain:

- Effects
- Properties
- Property Groups
- Settings
- Keyframes
- Expressions

Save Everything II

Animation presets can be applied to their originating comp or at any point in the future. That's because the presets are actually stored to a separate file on your hard drive (much like Photoshop Actions).

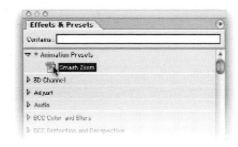

- If you save animation presets in the Favorites folder, they'll appear in the Effects & Presets Window.

- Be sure to back up your presets folder or a reinstall could blow away all of your custom work.

- All previous favorites from earlier versions are promoted to animation presets.

To create and save an animation preset:

❶ Choose the properties, property group, or effects (or any combo of these) that you want to keep and reuse.

❷ Choose Animation>Save Animation Preset or click the Save Animation button in the Effects & Presets palette.

❸ Give your preset a descriptive name and then add the extension .ffx

❹ Place the preset into the Favorite folder and if you'd like you can create subfolders to organize your effects. These subfolders will show up in the Effects & Presets palette.

ON THE SPOT

Master of Time:
Getting Results in the Timeline

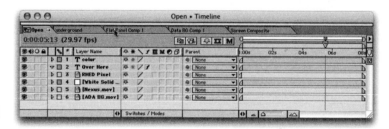

The Timeline is where all of the action happens. It's the window that gets your art from start to finish. The more you know about its nuances, the better your results will be.

In this chapter, we'll show you how to get the most out of your timeline, how to take advantage of its power, and how to do some tricks that will make…well…doing tricks easier.

The timeline in AE has always been flexible. And with After Effects 6.5, it has become a contortionist, bending over backward to make your life easier. Once you get comfortable with pre-composing, editing, resizing, and–well, you get the picture–you'll be the envy of designers everywhere.

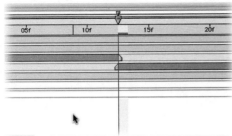

Breaking Up Is Easier

Often you will need to segment a layer. This might be for compositing purposes, such as making an object orbit around another. Other times it will make certain effects, such as Shatter. easier to control.

To split a layer, use the following steps:

❶ To split a layer, place the position indicator at the desired time.

❷ Select the layer to be split by highlighting it.

❸ Press Cmd+Shift+D (Ctrl+Shift+D).

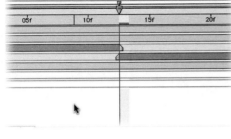

Make Your Mark (and Comment)

Layer Markers can come in handy when leaving notes to yourself within a composition. You can save time by adding the marker and calling up its dialog box with one key combination.

❶ To add a Layer Marker with dialog, press Option+* (the multiply symbol) on the numeric keypad.

❷ You can now add a comment, chapter marker, or Web link to your composition.

❸ Click OK when finished.

Under AE 6.5 you can now add layer markers while previewing in the Layer Window!

• This is an advantage as there are no previews to cache.

• Markers will also carry to multiple compositions when you add the footage item.

Get on Top

Next time you need to work on a layer, try these two shortcuts.

- On the numeric keypad, type the number of the layer you want to work with. For digits greater than 9, be sure to type the numbers quickly with no gap.

- Press X to Scroll the selected layer to the top of the Timeline view.

Mighty Mouse

Whether you run on a Mac or a PC, you need a two-button mouse with a scroll wheel to get the most out of After Effects 6.5. Powerful navigation shortcuts are now at your fingertips.

- The mouse wheel will scroll vertically in the Composition, Layer, or Footage Windows.

- Hold the shift key to scroll horizontally in the Timeline and Project windows.

- Hold the Option (Alt) key down to zoom around your mouse point in the Composition, Layer, or Footage windows. In the timeline, this shortcut lets you zoom in time.

- The Option (Alt) key will also zoom you around a selected track or mask point.

You don't have to have a window active, just hover over the window you want to pan, tilt, or zoom.

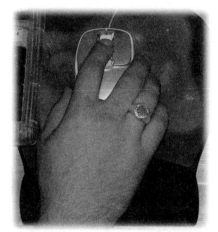

Lost Your Way

If you've ever been zoomed in on your Timeline, you know how easy it is to misplace the Current Time Indicator. You could Zoom the Timeline back out to find it, or scroll left or right as you search. But there's an easier way. (You knew we'd say that). Press D to scroll your Timeline View to the Current Time Indicator.

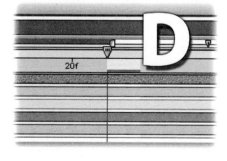

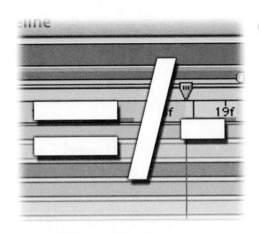

A Closer View I

Need to get a better look at your Timeline? You can quickly zoom in and out from the keyboard. Press = (equal sign) to Zoom In. Press − (minus sign) to Zoom Out. We just remember that the zoom in key has a plus sign on it.

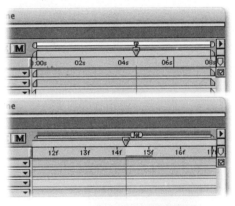

A Closer View II

Need an even closer view of your Timeline? The tightest view you can have is a frame level view. Why bother adjusting the Zoom slider, or even tapping the = key multiple times? You can toggle between a frame level view and your current zoom level by tapping the ; (semicolon) key.

Pick a Layer, Any Layer

Want to quickly pick a layer to work with? Just type its number on the numeric keypad. Type a single digit for layers 1–9. For higher levels, type the layer number such as 1 and 5 for 15.

Back to Keyframes

You just finished previewing your comp and it looks great, except for that one layer. A couple of quick tweaks to its keyframes and it would be perfect. You'll soon get tired of twirling down through each effect just to get to your keyframes. The fast way is to press U to toggle your Uber Animating Keyframes' view. Because we need all the help we can get, we think of this shortcut as U for User Keyframes.

The Fundamentals of Animation

There are five key components to animating a layer in After Effects. Fortunately, Adobe put these properties at your fingertips.

- Press A to Twirl down the Anchor Point.

- Press P to Twirl down the Position.

- Press R to Twirl down the Rotation.

- Press S to Twirl down the Scale.

- Press T to Twirl down the Opacity. (Think transparency.)

The following modifier keys also come in handy.

- Hold down the Shift key to display additional properties after selecting the first.

- Hold down the Option key to display a property and add a keyframe at the Current Time Indicator. On a PC, hold down Alt+Shift+ the shortcut letter (A, P, R, S or T) to achieve the same action.

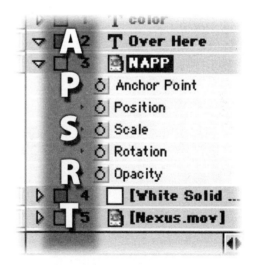

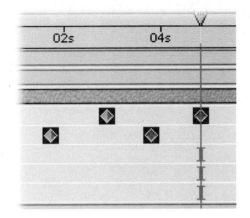

Get Those Keyframes

Need to select multiple keyframes? Here are a few tips to make it easier.

- Select all keyframes associated with a property by clicking on that property's name in the timeline.

- Add to that selection by Shift+Clicking on additional properties.

- Lasso visible keyframes in the Timeline window.

- Select all visible keyframes by pressing Cmd+Option+A (Ctrl+Alt+A).

- In 6.5 you can also deselect keyframes (while still leaving the layer highlighted. Press Cmd+Option+Shift+A (Ctrl+Alt+Shift+A) to deselect only keyframes and groups.

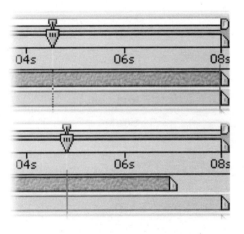

Nudge It

By now you've likely discovered that your arrow keys can be used to nudge footage in the Comp Window. Did you know that you can nudge in the timeline as well? Selected layers can be slid forward and backward from the keyboard.

- To Nudge a layer earlier, press Option+Page Up (Alt+Page Up).

- To Nudge a layer later, press Option+Page Down (Alt+Page Down).

- To Nudge a layer to even earlier frames, press Option+Shift+Page Up (Alt+Shift+Page Up).

- To Nudge a layer to even later frames, press Option+Shift+ Page Down (Alt+Shift+ Page Down).

A Different Kind of Nudge

Missing a beat? Do your elements seem just a little out of sync? A gentle nudge to a keyframe may be the answer. Select the desired keyframe by clicking on it.

- To Nudge a keyframe earlier, press Option+Left Arrow (Alt+Left Arrow).

- To Nudge a keyframe later, press Option+Right Arrow (Alt+Right Arrow).

- To Nudge a keyframe even earlier, press Option+Shift+Left Arrow (Alt+Shift+Left Arrow).

- To Nudge a keyframe even later, press Option+Shift+Right Arrow (Alt+Shift+Right Arrow).

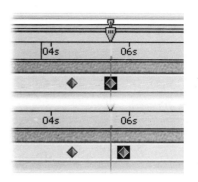

Step Inside the Box

At any point of time, you can step inside a pre-composition. By Option+double-clicking on a pre-comp, you can step inside. Any changes made to the pre-comp will be reflected in all compositions for which the pre-comp is a part.

What's in a Name?

A layer can have two names, the one it comes in with, and the one you give it. Why is this useful? It all boils down to you keeping control. Perhaps you have added a footage item five times into your composition. If every layer was called Shot 1, you might get confused. We would.

❶ Highlight the layer to rename it.

❷ Press Return (Enter).

❸ Type the new name.

❹ Press Return (Enter) to apply the name, or click on another layer.

If you'd like to toggle between all of the Source Names and the Layer Names, click the name field at the top of the timeline.

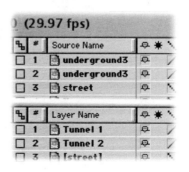

Keys to the Locks

You are your own worst enemy, so protect your comp. Want to avoid accidentally deleting or modifying a layer? Lock It! You can quickly lock a selected layer by pressing Cmd+L (Ctrl+L). But what if you change your mind? You can't use the same shortcut because locked layers cannot be selected. Here's what to do instead. Press Cmd+Shift+L (Ctrl+Shift+L) to Unlock All Layers.

Get There on Time

There are two ways to invoke moving the current time indicator, and that is, by clicking on the time counter in the timeline, or by pressing Cmd+G (Ctrl+G). Once the dialog box is open, there's a lot you can do with it.

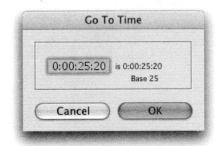

- Type in the time you'd like to go to. There is no need to type colons for the time. For example, you can just put 415 to move to the four and a half second mark using NTSC 29.97 fps counting.

- You can move forward a relative amount from your current position; simply type an amount such as +20 to move 20 frames forward.

- Conversely, you can move backward in time, but the phrasing is a little tricky. Open the Go To Time box and type in +–45 frames to move back 45 frames. While it seems confusing at first, you are saying "Add a negative adjustment to the current time."

- If you want to pre-roll an effect, you need to move to a time before your composition begins. Type in negative three seconds (–300) in the Go To Time box, your current time indicator. This way, particle effects or those that need to 'ramp up' have adequate time to begin.

Under After Effects 6.5, the Current Time field can also be scrubbed allowing you to shuttle through the timeline.

This Layer is Too Small

Have you ever wished for the power to tweak scale right from the keyboard? No twirling down three layers just to access the Scale sliders? You can adjust layer size quickly using the numeric keypad.

- To nudge scale larger, press Cmd+the plus sign on the numeric keypad (Ctrl+the plus sign on the numeric keypad).

- To nudge scale smaller press Cmd+the minus sign on the numeric keypad (Ctrl+the minus sign on the numeric keypad).

Add the Shift key to the above combinations to scale more quickly.

Send Your Layers Home

Want to get all your selected tracks lined up at the starting line? This will ensure a clean start to your composition and avoid any flash frames.

❶ Select any layers you want to align. You can Shift+Click to select a range of layers, or Cmd+Click (Ctrl+Click) to select noncontiguous layers.

❷ To align your layers to the start of the Comp, press Option+HOME (Alt+Home).

Alternately, this trick can work to line things up at the end of the comp as well. Just substitute Option+End (Alt+End) to align all layers to the rear of the comp.

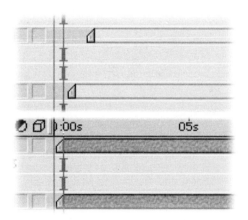

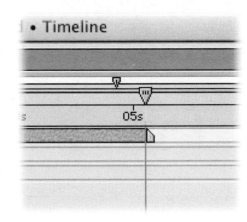

Making your Point (In or Out)

Need to move the in point or out point of a layer? No problem. You can avoid numeric entry all together and harness the power of the keyboard.

❶ Place the Current Time indicator at the desired time.

❷ To Set the Time In, press the [(left bracket) key. Or, To Set the Time Out, press the] (right bracket) key.

Using this method, you can set either an in or an out point, but not both.

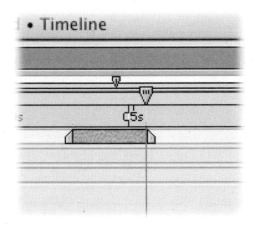

Making Two Points (In and Out)

Want to set both your in and out points for a layer? This can easily be accomplished in the Timeline Window.

❶ Place the Current Time indicator at the desired time.

❷ To set the Time In, press the [(left bracket) key. This will move the in-point to the Current Time indicator. If you'd like to trim earlier material, press Option+[(Alt+[ ) to Time Trim the in point.

❸ Move the Current Time indicator to the desired end time.

❹ To set the Time Trim for the out point, press Option+] (Alt+]).

I'd Like to Move in the Timeline

Need to move your Current Time Indicator around? It's easy to make small moves if you know the key combos. Be careful not to just tap the arrow keys, however. By themselves, the arrow keys nudge your footage in the composition window.

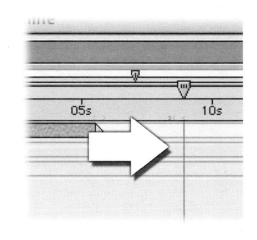

FUNCTION	MAC	PC
Time Step Forward	Cmd+Right Arrow or PgDn	Ctrl+Right Arrow or PgDn
Time Step Forward More	Shift+Cmd+Right Arrow or Shift+PgDn	Shift+Ctrl+Right Arrow or Shift+PgDn
Time Step Back	Cmd+Left Arrow or PgUp	Ctrl+Left Arrow or PgUp
Time Step Back More	Shift+Cmd+Left Arrow or Shift+PgUp	Shift+Ctrl+Left Arrow or Shift+PgUp

Boxes Inside of Boxes

When you go on a trip, do you just throw everything into your suitcase? Your toothbrush and toothpaste in the same compartment with your swimsuit, running shoes, dress shirts? If you do, I'm sure you've had a few surprises after the gorillas have thrown your bags around a bit. The organized traveler uses several small bags and pouches to keep belongings intact and looking their best. The same holds true in After Effects.

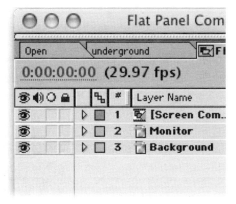

If your timeline has more than 20 layers, you should really consider organizing it better. Precomposing allows you to take several layers and put them into a new composition. They still live in your timeline, but are far easier to manage and track. To Pre-Compose, simply highlight the desired layers and press Shift+Cmd+C (Shift+Ctrl+C).

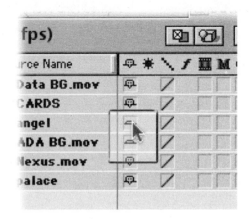

It's OK, Be Shy

Have a lot of layers in your timeline? Of course you do, you're smart and talented enough to be reading this advanced book. Wouldn't it be nice to make a little more room in your timeline to see things? Harness the Shy layers feature to dramatically cut down on vertical scrolling.

❶ To designate a layer as shy, click on the little "Kilroy" icon on each layer you want to hide.

❷ At the top of the timeline click the Shy (Kilroy) icon.

❸ All shy layers will disappear from the timeline view. They will, however, continue to affect the composition, and their results will show up in the Comp Window.

❹ At any time, you can reveal all shy layers by clicking on the Shy icon at the top of the timeline.

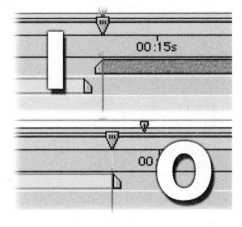

Get Me Out (Or In)

Need to quickly move to the start (or end) of a layer? Press I to jump to the In point of a layer, or O to jump to the Out point. Remember though, if a layer starts or ends outside of your composition's time range, you won't see the playhead (content) in After Effects.

If running AE 6.5, there's additional shortcuts between in and out points in your comp.

• Press Cmd+Shift+Option+Right Arrow (Ctrl+Shift+Alt+Right Arrow) to move to the next in or out point

• Press Cmd+Shift+Option+Left Arrow (Ctrl+Shift+Alt+Left Arrow) to move to the previous in or out point

Remapping Time

One of After Effects' least understood (and coolest) features has to be time remapping. Simply put, this awesome feature allows you to move frames of video around like they were keyframes.

❶ Select the layer you want to remap.

❷ Choose Layer>Enable Time Remapping or press Cmd+Option+T (Ctrl+Alt+T).

❸ You will now see a keyframe for the first frame of video and the last. You also now have the ability to extend the trim handle at the end of the shot indefinitely, but it will just create a freeze frame at the end of the video track.

❹ You can drag keyframes apart to slow the speed of motion; conversely you can shorten the distance between keyframes to speed the shot. Alternately, adjust the velocity controls up or down, and AE will automatically adjust the spacing of your keyframes.

❺ Additional keyframes can be added to create complex, variable speed-motion effects. Once added, keyframes can have their time value manipulated. For example, you can adjust values to an earlier time to create a rewind effect.

❻ To improve transitions in speed, use keyframe assistants for ease, or manually adjust the Bezier controls.

❼ If time values are remapped, you must enable frame blending for best results. Be sure to enable it globally at the top of the timeline and for the time remapped layers. Do not enable time remapping on other layers as it increases render time. Only footage layers, or precomps, can have their values remapped.

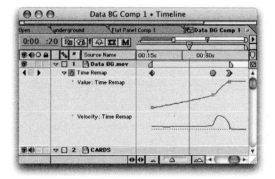

In Reverse

Want to quickly switch a layer's playback direction? Press Cmd+Option+R (Ctrl+Alt+R) to switch the playback direction. The key advantage to this method is that a layer's in and out points are preserved.

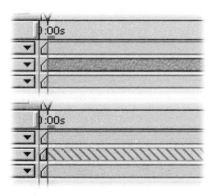

Getting Around the Keys

Need to move between your keyframes? Press K to move forward one keyframe. Press J to move back one keyframe. These shortcuts work with all visible keyframes, not just those on the selected layer.

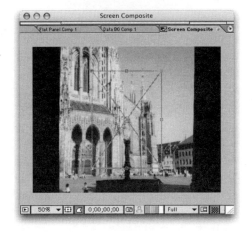

Size Matters

Have you ever tried to scale a really huge layer? Unless you like scaling in the Timeline, you've probably zoomed way out to 25 percent just so you can find the scale handles. Next time, try holding down the Option key (Alt key) and drag it anywhere within the layer in the Comp window. Drag toward the center to scale in; drag away from the center to scale out.

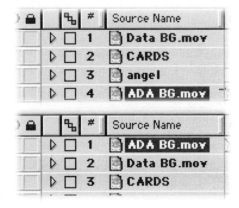

On Top of the Deck

While dragging layers around is often a valid option, it's not the fastest way to put a layer at the top of an 80-layer composition, especially if it's near the bottom. There are several keyboard shortcuts that will come in handy.

- To bring a layer to the front, press Cmd+Shift+] (Ctrl+Shift+]).

- To bring a layer to the back, press Cmd+Shift+[(Ctrl+Shift+[).

- To move a layer one spot closer to the top, press Cmd+] (Ctrl+]).

- To move a layer one spot farther back, press Cmd+[(Ctrl+[).

Got Snaps?

When dragging layers in the timeline, hold down the Shift key. This will invoke snapping to things like heads of clips and visible keyframes.

The Perfect Clone

While duplicating a layer is often as simple as pressing Cmd+D (Ctrl+D), sometimes you'll get unexpected results. If you want to duplicate a layer, you may accidentally end up duplicating a mask, or an effect applied to that layer. To avoid cloning mishaps, do this:

Press F2 to deselect all items. Click on the layer name you want to duplicate. Press Cmd+D (Ctrl+D).

A Better Timeline

There are several Optional Panels available in the timeline. If you'd like to add or subtract headings, simply Control click on any column heading, and pick from the list. If you don't like the column order, drag them left or right to new positions.

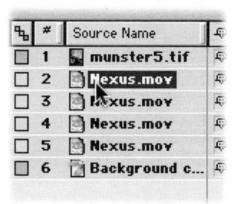

ON THE SPOT

AE in 3D:
Working in 3D Space

There are several ways to incorporate 3D into an AE Comp: you can cheat and use one of the perspective effects, like Basic 3D; you can use a plug-in with a built-in 3D engine, like Zaxwerks 3D invigorator or Shatter; you can import data from a 3D application, like Maya or 3D Studio Max; or you can animate with After Effect's built-in 3D engine, which is the focus of this chapter.

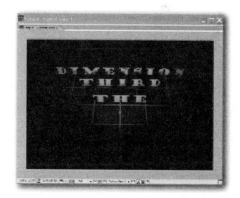

After Effect's 3D engine is sometimes referred to as "2.5D," or "postcards in space," because 3D layers have no depth (or extrusion). They are flat layers that can occupy and move around in 3D space, but if you turn them on their sides, you will see that they are flat like postcards.

Keeping this limitation in mind (or even using it to your advantage), you can use AE to generate beautiful, stylized effects, such as animations that look like pop-up books or text that flies off a printed page.

OpenGL and See What's Inside

If your video card and AE play nice together (you'll be able to tell if they don't if this tip doesn't work), you can use AE 6.0's new OpenGL renderer to display animating 3D layers faster.

- Click the OpenGL button at the bottom of the Comp Window. Select OpenGL with Static Textures if you're animating still images that are moving around in 3D space. Select OpenGL with Moving Textures if you're animating videos moving around in 3D space. Actually, you may want to choose the Static option even if you're animating videos, because the display will speed up even more, but video layers will freeze on their first frame.

- OpenGL speeds up display only while you're working in the Timeline. It does not speed up the final render. And you can't use it to RAM preview your animation. Still, it really speeds things up when you're dragging 3D layers around in the Comp Window, scrubbing the Current Time Indicator or hitting the spacebar to play.

- Most AE Effects won't display while OpenGL is active. The effects will still render, but you won't see them while you're viewing your Comp using OpenGL.

- To check which video cards play nice with After Effects, see http://www.adobe.com/products/aftereffects/opengl.html.

Z: 3rd Dimension or a Snore?

If you try to move a layer closer or further away in Z space, you may fall asleep before you're able to move the layer very far. By default, it moves in tiny increments, very slowly. But if you point to the Z-axis, start dragging, and then add in the Shift key. AE will swoosh your layer far away (or super close) very quickly.

Rotation Makes My Head Spin

When you want to rotate a 3D layer in the Comp, type W to switch to the Rotation tool. (V will switch you back to the Black Arrow selection tool when you're done.) Then choose Rotation or Orientation from the dropdown menu at the bottom of the Tools Palette.

Rotation is the best choice for animating. Orientation is better for posing. This is because when you keyframe Orientation, it always takes the shortest path between two angles. If you start with a layer rotated 0 degrees and orient it clockwise to 350 degrees, in the final animation, it will rotate counterclockwise from 0 to 350. On the other hand, Rotation remembers which direction you rotated the layer and how many times around you went.

65

My Name's Solid and I'm a 3D Layer

Do you ever wish your 3D layers could join groups? For instance, if you create a cube out of six 3D layers, using the 3D Assistants, how do you rotate the entire cube as a single object? Well, there are two ways.

- You could select one of the sides—maybe the front side—to be a parent to all of the other sides and then just rotate the parent. This solution works well when you want to move or rotate the entire cube as a single unit but also animate individual sides separately (maybe making the top of the box flip open). Children can always act independently from their parents (just like in read life!) So the layer that acts as the top of the box can flip up, no problem. But if you move, scale or rotate the parent, the children will go along for the ride.

- The other solution is to pre-compose all of the 3D layers you want to group together. Once they're flattened to a single layer, you must turn on both the Continually Rasterize switch (even if the layers are bitmaps), which is also called the Collapse Transformations switch, and the 3D switch

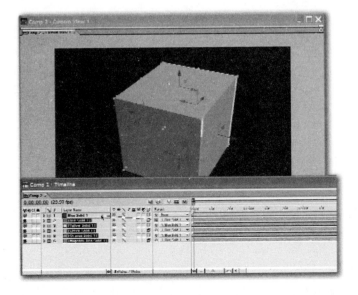
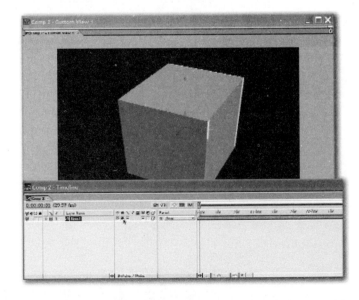

Smile, You're on Orbiting Camera!

Generally, to make one layer orbit around another, you drag the orbiting layer's Anchor Point onto the center of the layer it's orbiting around and animate Rotation. Alas, you can't do this with cameras, because they don't have Anchor Points.

But you can fashion a fake Anchor Point for your camera by using a Null Object and a little parenting.

❶ To create the Null Object, choose Layer>New>Null Object. Null Objects are layers that don't render.

❷ Turn on your Null's 3D switch and place it at the point you want the camera to rotate around (i.e., in the center of your 3D scene).

❸ Then animate the Null rotating in a complete circle (keyframe its X, Y or Z Rotation property).

❹ Finally, parent the camera to the Null and you'll get a lovely orbiting camera.

Optionally, you can animate the camera's position to make it gradually move closer to the Null as it orbits. That will give you a spiraling camera.

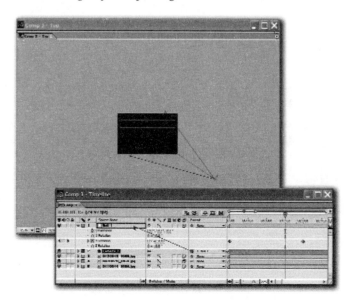

Try Seeing Things from My View

In full-fledged 3D programs like 3D Studio Max and Maya, you can see several views at once: top, left, front and perspective. You can do the same thing in After Effects!

❶ After adding some 3D layers to your Comp, choose View>New View.

❷ A new tab will appear in the Comp window. Drag the tab away from the Comp window until it becomes a second, floating Comp window.

❸ Set the camera view in this window to Top, and arrange two comp views any way you like.

❹ Go to View>New View two more times and create two more floating Comp windows with camera views Left and Front.

❺ Finally, choose Window>Workspace>Save Workspace. When AE prompts you for a name, type Four 3D Views. From now on, any time you want to bring up a Maya-like interface, you can choose Window>Workspace>Four 3D Views.

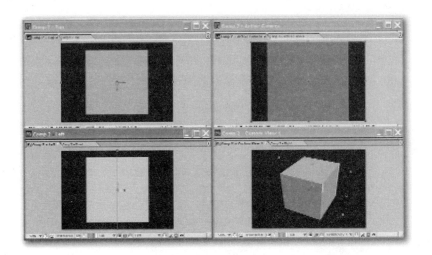

2D or not 2D, That Is the Question

2D layers act as impenetrable walls for 3D layers. If you want to create a bug (station identification) that always sits in the lower-right corner, and you don't want anything to ever obscure it, make your bug a 2D layer at the top of your layer stack. That way, no matter how far forward you bring 3D layers in Z-space, they'll never be able to get in front of the 2D layer.

Similarly, if you want a background that is guaranteed to always be the farthest layer back (maybe it's a star field, and you want to make sure that none of the spaceships ever move behind it), keep it a 2D layer and move it to the bottom of the stack.

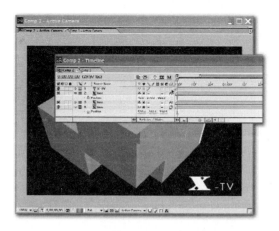

There's a Stain on My Window!

When you shine a light on a 3D layer, you can make the light pass through it just like sunlight passing through a stained-glass window. The light casts a shadow on any layers behind the stained-glass layer, and the shadow's color and shape will be taken from the layer it passes through.

❶ Remember to enable shadows for the light layer.

❷ Then twirl open the stained-glass layer's Material Options. Turn Cast Shadows on and set Pass Through to 100 percent.

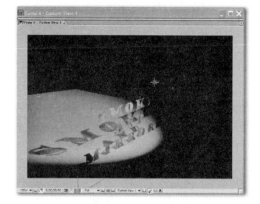

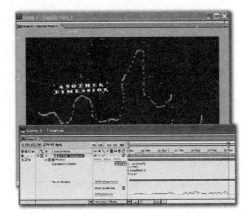

The Path to Righteousness—in 3D

By adding a simple expression to a layer's Position property, you can turn a 2D motion path into a 3D motion path.

First create the path via keyframing, pasting a path from Illustrator, or using Motion Sketch. Then turn on the layer's 3D switch, and add the following expression to its Position property:

$X = position[0];$

$Y = 200;$

$Z = position[1];$

$[X,Y,Z]$

Command (Control). Scrub at a slower speed when adjusting values.

Shift. Change scrubbing at a higher value.

When the layer was 2D, the path moved it around the X and Y dimensions. This expression will change movement to the X and Z dimensions. Whenever it formerly moved up and down (Y), it will now move in and out (Z). Its up and down movement will be constrained to 200 pixels from the top of the Comp window. Change the number 200 if you want the Y position to be elsewhere. If you want the movement to occur in the Y and Z axes, change the expression to the following:

$X = 200;$

$Y = position[1];$

$Z = position[0];$

$[X,Y,Z]$

It's Good to Be Blurry

Perhaps the coolest feature of AE's 3D cameras is the Depth of Field option. This makes objects out of a camera's range (too close or too far) appear blurred, just as they would with a real camera.

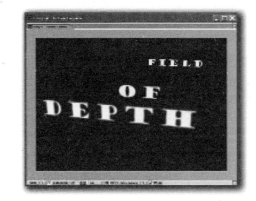

❶ To try it out, press Cmd+Option+C (Ctrl+Alt+C), or, if you want to be ordinary, choose Layer>New>Camera from the menu.

❷ In the New Camera dialogue, select a narrow angle preset, like 80mm (the larger the mm number, the narrower the angle–small numbers are for wide-angle lenses).

❸ Also, make sure the Depth of Field option is enabled. In the Timeline, you can adjust the strength of the Depth of Field effect by twirling open the camera layer, then twirling open the Options and adjusting the Blur Level.

I'm the Active Camera! No, I Am

You can add multiple cameras to your 3D Comp, but only one of their views can render at a time. From the Comp window's 3D view menu, you can select any camera you want to look through while you're working, but only the Active Camera will render. So how do you make a specific camera the Active Camera?

By placing it on top of the layer stack. The highest up camera will always be the Active Camera. If you want to cut between two cameras, place the first camera on top, but make it end partway through the Comp's duration. (Drag its out-point to the left, so that it doesn't extend all the way to the end of the Comp). When the first camera-layer ends, it will no longer be the topmost camera; the next camera down in the stack will become the Active Camera.

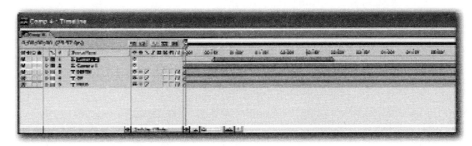

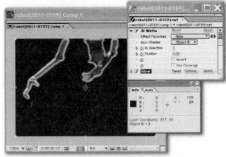

May I See Your ID Please?

If you want to isolate one object in your 3D scene and apply an effect to it (i.e. placing a glow around the robot but not around the spaceship), apply the ID Matte effect (in the 3D Channel category).

❶ Click a pixel in the robot and note its ID number in the Info Palette.

❷ Then change the ID Selection parameter (in the ID Matte effect) to match the ID number from the Info Palette.

❸ After Effect will display the robot and mask out everything else. You can then apply any effect to they layer and it will only affect the robot.

❹ To add back the rest of the scene, place a second copy of the original scene (spaceship and robot) below the robot layer.

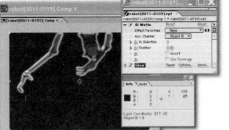

Man, Those Layers Are Stacked!

We all know that when working in 2D, we all know that the highest layer in the Timeline is in front of all the other layers, and the lowest layer is behind them, but when you make the layers 3D, their order in the Timeline stack becomes much less important.

- 3D layers are stacked by their Z-position value (assuming the camera is pointing at their fronts). Therefore, So the layer closest to the Active camera is in front of all the other layers, even if that layer is way down low in the Timeline stacking order.

- There are a few exceptions to this rule: Track Matte layers must still be on top of the layer they are masking.

- Layer blend modes still respect the stacking order in the Timeline. However, only the Advanced 3D renderer will properly blend intersecting layers in the blended layer functions in 3D space.

- 2D layers also are also ordered by their place in the Timeline stack.

- If several 3D layers share the exact same Z-position value, AE will use their Timeline stacking order to determine which one is on top.

Don't Bruise the Material

If you shine a light on a 3D layer, you can affect how the light interacts with the layer by adjusting its Material Options.

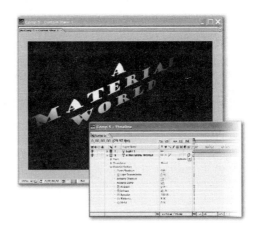

❶ Twirl open the layer that is being hit by the light (not the light layer), and then twirl open the Material Options category. The key properties to adjust are Ambient, Diffuse, Specular, Shininess, and Metal.

❷ To get a sense of how they work, drill them all down to zero, and then experiment by scrubbing each one up, one by one.

❸ Start with Spectacular, which will add a hotspot to your layer. When you first raise this value, it may turn your whole layer into one big hotspot.)

❹ Then raise Shininess, which makes your hotspot smaller and dims out the rest of the layer.

❺ Next, raise the Diffuse property, which will fill in the darker areas (the areas not in the hotspot).

❻ Raising metal will lower the color distinction between the darker areas and the highlight, but the highlight will still be brighter.

❼ Raising the Ambient property makes the layer look slightly more reflective, but the difference is pretty subtle compared with the other Material Option properties

Fine. Don't Use My Camera!

Many Effects, like Shatter, have their own built-in 3D systems, complete with cameras and lights, but if you're comfortable using AE's lights and camera (or if you want those effects to blend into an AE 3D scene), you can use them instead of the ones built into the effects. Just check the "Use Comp Camera" or "Use Comp Lights" option in the Effect's property list. Don't enable the 3D switch for the layer with the effect applied to it (i.e., the Shatter layer).

Effects that can use AE's cameras and lights include Shatter, Wave World, Card Dance and Zaxwerks 3D Invigorator.

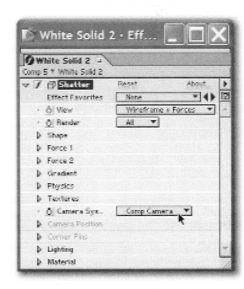

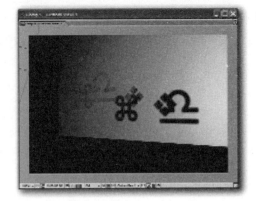

The Shadow Knows

So you've added a light layer to your 3D Comp and checked the Cast Shadows option in the Light Settings dialogue. If you forgot to do this, select the light layer, choose Layer>Light Properties from the menu, and check the option).,

But still, you don't see any shadows.

That's because AE tries its darndest to stop you from using shadows, which are (they're very cruel to your computer's processor). It's not enough to enable shadows on the light layer. All of the other layers also need Cast Shadows enabled before you'll see any shadows. So select all of your 3D layers (except lights and cameras), and on any one of the selected layers, twirl open its Material Options. Click the word "off" by Cast Shadow to change it to "on."

Don't turn Cast Shadows on for any layers that won't be casting shows. For instance, your background layer won't cast shadows, because there isn't another layer behind it to receive any shadows it might cast). Turning on Cast Shadows for these layers just needlessly increases render time, because AE will calculates the shadows even though it doesn't display them.

You Can Call Me Ray

So you've tried pointing an AE light directly at the active camera, hoping to see rays bursting out of it. But instead, you got darkness. What gives? Light that emits rays is called "volumetric light." (Think of light that fills up a volume), and unfortunately AE's lights aren't volumetric. This is where third-party plug-ins come to the rescue. Three popular ones for creating rays of light are Trapcode's Shine and Lux as well as Red Giant's Knoll Light Factory.

Manipulating the Manipulators

When you turn on a layer's 3D switch, the most noticeable change is the appearance of the "manipulators" at the center of the layer. Dragging these red, green and blue arrows allow you to Constrain-Drag (or Constrain-Rotate, if you're using the Rotate tool) a layer in the X, Y or Z directions.

- The three Axis Mode buttons on the Tool Palette dictate which way is X, which way is Y and which way is Z. The default Axis mode is Local, which means that each layer has its own X, Y and Z. Rotate a layer around its Y axis (so that you're staring at its edge, like a postcard), and its Z axis will no longer point straight at you. It will point to the right or to the left (like the X axis used to), depending on which way you rotated the layer. In Local Axis Mode, you can think of the manipulator as being attached to the layer, and rotating with it.

- Contrast that with World Axis Mode, which is the middle Axis Mode button on the Tool Palette: in World Axis Mode, no matter how you rotate the layer, the manipulators stay put. This is because World Axis Mode uses set X, Y and Z directions. This is similar to the real world, in which North is always North. If you change your view by moving the active camera or selecting one of the view options in the Comp Window (i.e., Top or Custom View 1), the manipulators will change direction. But they will still point to "true" X, Y and Z. Similarly, if you were in a space ship, hovering over the North Pole, north would be below you.

- The final option, View Axis Mode, orients to your screen. So that no matter how you move the camera or layer, X always points left and right, Y always points up and down, and Z always points in and out.

Camera Shy

Are you scared of cameras? In After Effects, when you add a camera layer, the most frightening dialogue window (except maybe the Particle Playground Effect Controls) appears.

The settings in this window are great, if you want to mimic a real-world camera (and if you know how a real-world camera works). But for us Average Joes who just want to make some 3D text fly around, the best way to simplify the dialogue is to choose a camera preset.

- Lower numbers, such as 15mm, will give you a wide-angle lenses (taking in more of the view, but somewhat distorted).

- Higher numbers, like 80mm, will give you a narrow angle lenses.

- 50mm is a good default for a "normal" camera look.

- After adding a camera, you can always mess with the angle (as in "wide" or "narrow") by adjusting the Zoom property in the Timeline.

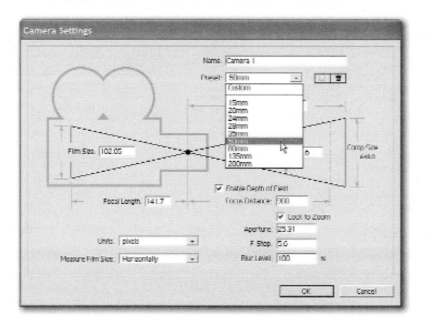

My Picture Got Panned!

Have you ever tried to pan an AE camera from left to right? If so, you've probably animated its Position so that it moved across the X dimension (or Y, if you're panning it up and down).

When you viewing your comp, you may be surprised to see that the camera move is a curvy path– not a straight left to right pan. Although the Position is changing, this is because , the Point of Interest is staying in the same place.

Cameras always point towards their Point of Interest, and as the camera moves, it turns to face its Point of Interest, which is what creates the curvy motion. To get a straightforward pan, turn the stopwatches on for both the Position and the Point of Interest properties before animating Position.

You don't need to animate Point of Interest. Just turn on its stopwatch on. Then, as you move the camera (animating its position), AE will automatically keyframe Point of Interest for you.

What's Your Point?

Do Points of Interest (on camera and light layers) confuse you? They're not that hard to understand. A camera or light's Point of Interest is a spot in 3D space (with an X, Y and Z position) where the camera or light is pointing. On the other hand, the camera or light's Position is where it's pointing from.

Still, confused? Okay, well, then you might want to get rid of the Point of Interest altogether.

❶ Select your camera or light layer and then choose Layer>Transform>Auto-orient from the menu.

❷ In the Auto Orientation dialogue, select the Off option. Now your camera or light will simply point at whatever it's rotated towards (adjust the Orientation and Rotation properties to change what the camera or light is pointing at).

Although normally the camera's Point Of Interest will move when you drag the camera around in the Comp Window, if you hold down the Command (Control) key after you start dragging the camera, you'll adjust only the camera's position while its Point of Interest remains where in place.

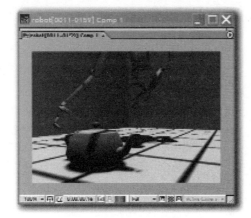

Importing Without a Tariff

As an alternative to using AE's 3D layers (which, alas, have no depth), you can import data from most popular 3D modeling and animation programs, such as Maya, 3D Studio Max, Softimage, Lightwave, Electric Image and Cinema4D.

In the 3D software, you'll have to export your scene as a PIC, RLA, RPF or EI. When you do so, make sure you enable options to save additional pixel information besides just red, green, blue and alpha. For instance, if your 3D app saves information about how far each pixel is away from the camera in Z-space, After Effects will be able to interpret that data.

For most of these image formats, the extra data is saved directly in the image files. The exceptions are Softimage's PIC files and Electric Image's EI files, which store the 3D data in additional files, ZPIC files for Softimage and EIZ files for Electric Image.

After Effects can still read this data. Don't import the ZPIC and EIZ files into After Effects. Instead place these files in the same folders as their associated PIC or EI files, and only import the PIC or EI into After Effects.

Importing Without a Tariff II

Once you've imported files from a 3D program and added them to your comp, you can access their 3D data by applying AE's 3D Channel Effects.

Before applying these effects, make sure you open the Info Palette (Window>Info).

Then, after applying a 3D Channel effect, click any pixel in the image to see its 3D data displayed in the Info Palette.

Wipe Your Feet on the 3D Matte

Most of the 3D channel effects create mattes, which are (grayscale images in which black represents transparent pixels, gray represents partially transparent pixels, and white represents opaque pixels). You can then use these images as track mattes that hide parts of the 3D data and reveal other parts of it.

Say you import a 3D animation of a car moving towards the camera. You'd like to insert a 2D image of some smoke halfway through the car's journey, so that it starts behind the smoke, drives through it and ends in front of the smoke.

To achieve this effect, you'd apply a 3D channel effect like 3D Channel Extract to the car layer. Then you'd click with your mouse at the point where you want the smoke to appear (halfway back into the scene). After clicking, you can read the Z position of this point in the Info Palette.

Adjust the Black Point and White Point properties in the 3D Channel Extract effect properties, until you get a matte in which the white starts where you want the fire to begin and ends at the camera. Everything behind the fire line should be black.

Arrange your Timeline with the layers stacked from top to bottom as follows: matte layer, copy of original car layer, smoke layer, and another copy of the car layer. Notice that the matte layer was made with a copy of the car layer, so the car layer will appear three times in the comp). Use the matte layer as a luma matte for the layer immediately below it.

In the comp, it will appear as if the car is passing through the smoke.

Use Advanced 3D Without a Ph.D.

After Effects ships with two 3D rendering plug-ins that controlling how 3D layers interact. You can access these by choosing Composition>Composition Settings or pressing Cmd+K (Ctrl+K). From the Composition Settings Window, click on the Advanced Tab and choose one of the following Rendering Plug-Ins.

Advanced 3D: By default, AE6 uses the Advanced 3D rendering plug-in. This plug-in accurately handles layer intersections (including blend modes and adjustment layers). It also uses shadow maps to give more control over shadow rendering.

Standard 3D: This was the original method that was introduced with AE5. You can use this if there are no intersecting layers. The benefit is that it's faster for some compositions. If rotated layers appear jaggy, click the Options button and choose the More Accurate anti-aliasing option.

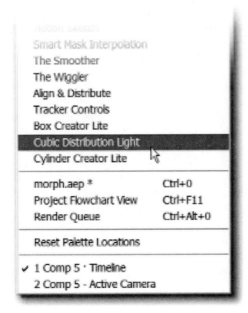

3D Assistants

On your After Effects 6 Install CD, you will find an installer from Digital Anarchy for 3D Assistants Lite. These three Assistants are a taste of the larger package of 3D Assistants available at www.DigitalAnarchy.com. These light versions however are fully functional, in fact we've invited Jim Tierney, Lead Anarchist of Digital Anarchy to show us how to use them in the next few tips.

3D Assistants I: Cylinder

By Jim Tierney, Digital Anarchy

❶   Start off with an initial nine layers. These can be footage or solid layers.

❷   We need to set up some properties of layers so that when we duplicate them we don't have to go back and try and change a property for 300 layers.

     a. Make all the layers 3D.

     b. Select the Best Quality check box, or leave it at Draft Quality just to speed things.

     c. With all the layers selected, open up the Material Options and turn on casting shadows.

     d. We want all layers to transmit light. Add an expression to each layer – except for the top layer. Option (Alt) click each layer's Material Options>Light Transmission property and then Pickwhip the top layer's Light Transmission property. This way, we'll be able to adjust all of the layer's Light Transmission via the top layer's Light Transmission.

❸   Now that we have the parameters set up let's duplicate the layers two times giving us 27 layers. Make sure that the layers are set up sequentially so that they repeat in a pattern in the Cylinder.

❹   At this point we need to point the two duplicated 'top' layers' Light Transmission property at the original 'top' layer's Light Transmission property. So add expressions to the duplicated 'top' layers Light Transmission properties and Pickwhip the one on the original top layer.

❺   Now we can start working on our Cylinder.

Choose Window>Cylinder Creator Lite and let's enter the following values:

Y: 4000 4000

Radius Set By First: 36 First: 36

Distance Between Layers Vertically: 517 517

Repeat Layers: 10 10

Repeat Sequentially: checked

❻   Click the apply button at the bottom of the Cylinder Creater Lite dialogue w.

❼   Now add a camera to the comp and zoom it back far enough so that you can see the who cylinder.

❽   Add a couple of lights to the comp. Try placing a point light inside the cylinder and a spotlight (pointing at the cylinder) outside it.

❾   Adjust the top layer's Light Transmission property until you like the effect.

3D Assistants II: Lights

By Jim Tierney, Digital Anarchy

While Lights exist in 3D space, they aren't technically 3D layers. This means you can't use the 3D Assistants to setup or animate a large number of lights. However, you can attach lights to Null objects, which can be 3D Layers. That means you can use lights with the 3D assistants, provided that the lights are parented to null objects.

Note: this tip assumes you've assembled the cylinder from the previous tip.

Let's try and pull this off.

1 Create a light with the following settings:

Type: Spot

Intensity: 80

Cone Angle: 90

Cone Feather: 70

2 Now create a null object. Make the null object 1 pixel by 1 pixel in size and then turn on the 3D switch. This creates a 3D null object, which we can now attach the light to.

3 Set the light position to match the null object position exactly. This will essentially put the light on top of the null object. Now parent the light to the null object.

4 Duplicate the light and null object five times, and link each light with its associated null object.

5 That gives us six lights to orient around the Cylinder. We are going to orient them around the outside because the panels should be letting the light through and the lights will illuminate the panels.

6 Select the 6 null objects and choose Window>Cylinder Creator Lite. Set it up with the following settings and click Apply:

X: 3000

Y: 20

Z: 3000

Distance Between Layers Vertically: Doesn't matter

Frequency of Layers Around Cylinder: 60 degrees

And just like that, we have used the 3D assistants to arrange our lights.

3D Assistants III: Nulling Nulls

By Jim Tierney, Digital Anarchy

Nulls are incredibly versatile animation assistants. Not only can they be used to control other layers, but they can be used to control other nulls. If we want to use a null to animate our lights en mass, we need to attach the null to the nulls controlling the lights, not the lights themselves.

❶ Create a new null that is in a center of the comp, which should put it in the center of the circle of lights. Turn on the null's 3D switch.

❷ Now select all the nulls that control the lights, then parent them to the new null.

❸ We want the lights to slowly move down the Cylinder and rotate as they're doing so. To do this, we will now just move the main null up to the top of the Cylinder. All lights will follow the main Cylinder up and we will set at a key frame for position and rotation of the main null.

❹ We now move the Current Time Indicator to the end of the time line and move the null down to the bottom of the Cylinder. This will automatically set another key frame for position, and then we can set a keyframe for Y rotation: 1x135.

❺ If we play this back, you can see the lights animating around the Cylinder.

❻ We can also make some adjustments here allowing some of the lights to cast shadows and vary the intensity and color of some of the lights.

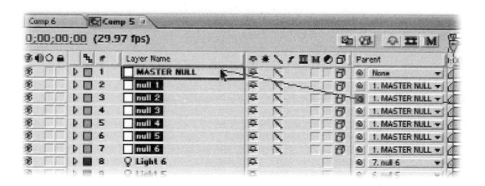

3D Assistants IV: Nulling Layers

By Jim Tierney, Digital Anarchy

If you have close to 300 layers you may need some help animating all of them:

❶ Create another 1 pixel by 1 pixel null in the center of the Cylinder.

❷ Turn on the Null's 3D switch.

❸ Select all of the layers. Make sure you did not select any of the lights or nulls.

❹ With all layers selected grab the parenting Pickwhip and select the Layer null. This will select the null object as the parent of all the layers selected. Making it very easy to attach a large number of layers to a single null.

❺ After parenting all the layers to the null object, set a keyframe for the Y rotation parameter of the null object at the beginning of the time line.

❻ Move to the end of the time line and set the Rotation to –1 X 0.0.

And that is it. We now have lights rotating around the Cylinder. And the Cylinder itself is rotating in the opposite direction. With everything controlled by null objects.

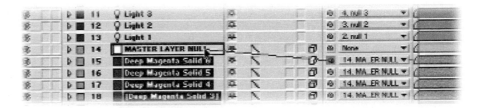

3D Assistants V: Exploding Layers

By Jim Tierney, Digital Anarchy

Using the Cubic Distribution assistants you can have a bunch of layers start off in a cluster and explode in random directions.

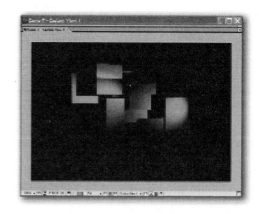

1 Select some 3D layers and choose Window>Cubic Distribution Lite.

2 Set the Cube Dimensions to 1 pixel by 1 pixel by 1 pixel. When you click apply this will position all the layers in basically the same place, creating a compact cluster of the layers.

3 Before you click apply, though, select Random under the Layer Orientation options and turn on Set Keys for Position and Orientation. You'll want the Cubic Distribution assistant to set keyframes for all the layers so they animate when their positions and rotations change.

4 Click Apply. The layers are thrown together in a cluster.

5 Move forward in time some amount, say, maybe 3 seconds.

6 Change the Cube Dimensions to 2000 pixels by 2000 pixels by 2000 pixels. Re-apply the assistant.

7 This will cause the layers to be distributed over a much larger area, creating an explosion of layers when you play the animation back.

3D Assistants VI: Line 'Em Up

By Jim Tierney, Digital Anarchy

If you want to line up all your layers in a straight line, you can use the Cubic Distribution assistant to do this easily.

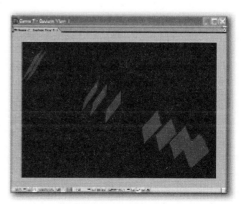

1 Set the Cubic Dimensions to be X = 1, Y= 1, and Z = 2000 (or however long you want). You now have created a very thin, very long cube that the layers will be distributed in. Of course, the only axis they can be distributed along is the Z-axis.

2 When you click apply, this results in all the layers being lined up in a straight line. Since the Cubic Distribution assistant distributes the layers randomly, they won't be evenly spaced, but they will be aligned evenly on the X and Y-axis.

Hold Shift For Real Time Feedback

by Zax Dow

Here's a real quick tip that helps when setting up the shapes of the models. By holding down the Shift key, sliders will give you real time feedback.

Say for instance, that you are adjusting the thickness of the objects. This is done with the Depth slider. Usually you drag the slider to a point then let go and the model rebuilds so you can see what the effect of the slider is. However, if you hold down the Shift key the model will rebuild while you are dragging the slider. This lets you home in on the look that you want much faster.

Shift-dragging is also a way to help get the creative juices flowing. You can try things that you might not think of doing, but because it is so easy you'll just try it anyway to see what happens. So the next time you are working on a project try dragging the Depth slider so the objects are really fat, then try dragging the other way to make them really thin. You might find that there is a setting that takes your design in a different direction.

Creative Zig-Zags

by Zax Dow

As mentioned in the tip on shift-dragging the Depth slider, you can sometimes bump into combinations of settings that help your design in ways that you might not expect. Here are some other settings to play with...

Object Faceting—By dragging this slider to the far right the objects will become very faceted, meaning that circles become square-ish and curves look like they've been rough-cut out of rock. The look is especially cool with italicized text.

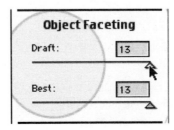

Spike Buster—By dragging this slider above the 90 degree mark, the corners of your objects will get clipped off as if you used a pair of scissors on them. This adds more angles to catch light and gives the objects a more detailed look.

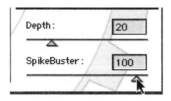

Edge Profiles—Try an Edge Profile that you've never tried before. Once you've picked a new profile you can use the keyboard's arrow keys to step through the profile list trying variation after variation. Some profiles are made for thin objects and others are made for thick objects, so if suddenly the objects look too fat and bloated just Shift-drag the Depth slider and to reveal the coolness within.

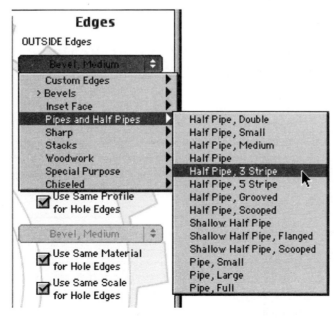

Turn Off The Faces—Turning off the front face of your objects will create "bowl" objects which look really cool when shadows from the sides fall onto the inside of the objects. Turning off the front and back faces will create hollow objects. Removing the faces creates an extra level of detail that can make a design say something new.

Fortunately it's really easy to try. One click to turn them off and another to turn them back on if you don't like the effect.

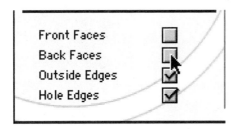

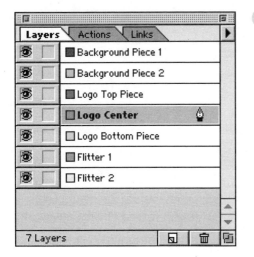

Instant Updates To Your 3D Models

by Zax Dow

By far one of the best features in the Invigorator is the ability to link each 3D model to the original Illustrator file that it came from. Once this link is made, changes to the Illustrator vector art will update the 3D objects within the Invigorator. In other words this feature will let you change the shape of your 3D objects without having to re-import the file, reapply the surface settings, or even reanimate the objects once they've been changed. It is the perfect tool for responding to the changes that occur during the course of a project.

The "file-model" linking is accomplished by following these easy steps:

Build the Illustrator file so that each object is placed on its own layer in Illustrator. An object can be made of more than one path. For instance, the word "hello" is made of many paths, but if all the letters are placed on a single layer, then during the next step they will all become a single object.

Open the Illustrator file in the Invigorator with the "Open By Layers" option turned ON. This will make each layer in the Illustrator file its own 3D object.

That sets up the magic. To make the magic happen do the following:

Make changes to the artwork in Illustrator, but don't move the artwork to a new layer. Keep the artwork on the same layer as it was when first brought into the Invigorator. Save the file.

Inside the Invigorator select the objects you want to update. Then click the Reload button on the Object tab. This will tell the Invigorator to find the original Illustrator file, look through it to find the layer that the object originally came from, and update the 3D model with the new vectors it finds in the edited file.

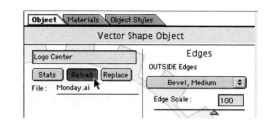

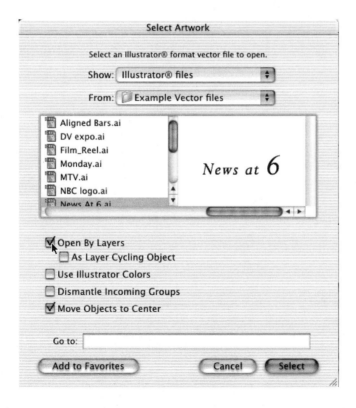

ON THE SPOT

Type-Oh:
Great Titles with AE's new Text Engine

When we got our copies of AE 6, the single feature that made us most impatient to rip the shrink-wrap off the package was the new Type Tool. Yes, you can now grab this tool, that sits innocently in the Tool Palette, click in the Comp Window and type—just like in Photoshop or Illustrator.

After Effects used to be weak in the text department. To achieve complex text-based animation, especially if we needed to animate text character-by-character, we turned to third-party plugins like Boris Graffiti or Digital Anarchy's Text Anarchy suite. Now we only need After Effects, which is now, in our opinion, the most advanced text-animation tool on the market.

But with power comes complexity. The rules for animating text are different from any other sort of animation in After Effects. This chapter will help you sort out your Ps from your Qs, and by the time you're done reading it, you'll think text is as easy as ABC.

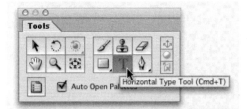

Adding Text to a Comp is Easy!

Press Cmd+T (Ctrl+T) to select the Horizontal Type tool. (Repeat this shortcut to toggle between the Horizontal Type tool and the Vertical Type tool).

Click anywhere in the Comp window and start typing.

When you finish, press the Enter key on the numeric keypad to exit typing mode. Note that pressing Return (Enter) on the main keyboard won't finalize your type. Instead, it will drop your type cursor down to the next line, just like in a word processor. If you're working on a laptop without a numeric keypad, you can finalize your type by clicking anywhere outside the Comp window (i.e., the Timeline) or selecting another tool (i.e., the Selection tool).

After Effects will create a Type Layer to hold all your text. This is a new type of layer added in AE 6.0. The type layer will be automatically named after the text you type. (If you type "Hello," the layer will be named "Hello.") You can change its name the same way you'd change any layer name: by selecting the layer name in the Timeline and pressing Return (Enter) and inserting the new name.

Centering Text Around a Point

When you drag a paragraph text bounding area, you scale it out from its upper-left corner. If you'd rather center it around a point, Option (Alt) and drag when you create it. The bounding box will grow out in all directions from the point where you started dragging.

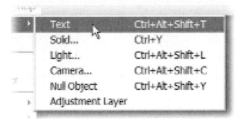

Centering Text in the Comp Window

If you create a text layer by choose Layer>New>Text from the menu, AE will place an insertion point (text cursor) at the exact center of the Comp window. Your text will be automatically centered.

Keyboard shortcut: Cmd+Option+Shift+T (Ctrl+Alt+Shift+T).

Point Text vs. Paragraph Text

When wielding the Type tool, you can create a text layer in one of two ways. Either click in the Comp window (to create Point Text), or hold the left mouse button down and drag in the Comp window (to create Paragraph Text).

Point Text treats each line you type as a separate block of text. New lines will only be created when your press the Return (Enter) key.

Paragraph Text wraps text around to the next line when your type reaches the edge of the current line. The edge–the text's bounding box– is defined by how far you dragged the mouse when you created the paragraph text layer. You can resize the bounding box (for Paragraph Text only) by selecting the text using the Type tool, clicking to place a cursor within the text, then dragging on one of the sizing handles around the perimeter of the bounding box. Shift-dragging a sizing handle will constrain the proportions of the bounding box. Make sure you don't accidentally drag a sizing handle with the Selection tool, or you'll scale the text, not its bounding box.

After Effects 6.5 you can convert between horizontal and vertical text. Make sure the text layer is not in editing mode.

❶   Select the Type tool

❷   Contextual click within the text layer.

❸   Choose Horizontal or Vertical, then adjust after AE changes the block.

Where's My Text?

When typing on a Paragraph Text layer, it's possible to add more text than can fit inside the bounding box. If you do this (or if you resize the bounding box so it's too small for the text you added earlier), After Effects will hide some of the text. The overflow symbol indicates there's hidden text. To reveal hidden text, either decrease the font size (so more of the text fits in its bounding area) or increase the size of the bounding area (using the Type tool). When the overflow symbol vanishes, there's no more hidden text.

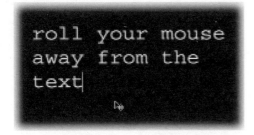

Moving Text with the Type Tool

You can drag text to a new location in the Comp Window without switching from the Type tool to the Selection tool. Just roll your mouse until the cursor is a little ways away from the text. The cursor will change from an I-bar to an arrow pointer. When you see this change, hold down the mouse button and drag the text to move it.

Or, with the Type tool selected, hold down the Cmd (Ctrl) key to temporarily switch to the Selection tool.

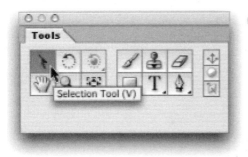

Selecting Text

Before you can adjust text properties (i.e., font size or text color), you must first select the text using either the Selection Tool or the Type tool.

The selection tool will select the entire text layer. Any adjustments you make will affect all of the characters. If you want to alter just some of the characters, highlight them with the Type tool (the same way you select text in a word processor).

Double clicking a text layer in the Comp window will highlight all of the text and switch you to the Type tool. You can type to replace current with new text. This is useful when you want multiple text layers, each with the same formatting choices but with different text. Use Cmd+D (Ctrl+D) to duplicate one text layer, drag the copies to different locations in the Comp window, then double-click each copy to change its text.

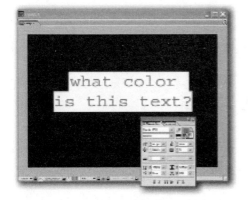

Turning off the Highlight

When text is highlighted. it's hard to see some of its formatting correctly, especially color choices. After selecting text, you can turn off highlighting (while still leaving the text selected) by using the keyboard shortcut Cmd+Shift+H (Ctrl+Shift+H). Repeat the same shortcut to toggle highlighting back on.

Changing Properties I

You can adjust text properties several ways. In the Character and Paragraph palettes:

type new values for properties (i.e., you can type a new numerical value in the font size input field).

- Click the little spinners (small arrow icons) next to numerical fields to incrementally increase or decrease values.

- Highlight the value in any input field, then use the up and down keyboard arrows to increase or decrease the current value. Shift Up Arrow and Shift Down Arrow will increase or decrease numerical values in steps of 10 (i.e., font size 20 will change to font size 30).

- The highlight method is especially effective when picking a font. Highlight the current font name, then use the Up and Down arrows to cycle through the list of installed fonts. Your selected text will change fonts each time when you press one of the arrow keys. You can jump to a specific font in your list of installed fonts by typing its name in the font field.

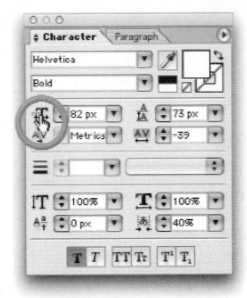

Changing Properties II: Scrubbing

The coolest way to adjust text properties is to scrub the little icons to the left of the property fields. For instance, you can adjust font size by clicking the icon that looks like a T with a cast shadow. Don't release the mouse after clicking. Instead, hold down the mouse button and drag to the left or the right, as if you're trying to drag the icon off the Character Palette. Dragging to the left will interactively decrease the font size; dragging to the right will increase it.

This feature is so cool, Adobe has also added it to Photoshop CS and Illustrator CS.

The Kerning Shortcut

Kerning means adjusting the spacing between pairs of letters. When font sizes are large, you'll often notice that the space between some letters seems wider or narrower than the spaces between other letters.

To even up the spacing, you can kern by placing your cursor between two letters, holding down the Option (Alt) key, then pressing the Left Arrow key to move the letters closer together or the Right Arrow key to move letters further apart. Since you can also use the Left and Right Arrow keys (without the Option or Alt key held down) to move the text cursor, you can quickly make many kerning adjustments by moving the cursor with the Arrow keys and adding in the Option (Alt) key when you want to kern.

Changing Text Over Time

Sometimes it's useful to make a sequence of words or sentences appear one after the other, in the same place, in the same font (i.e., for subtitles).

❶   Use the Type tool to type the initial text. Make careful font and style choices before continuing to the next step, because after adding keyframes, you'll have to redo the formatting adjustments at each keyframe.

❷   Twirl open the text layer in the timeline to reveal its properties.

❸   Twirl open the Text property group.

❹   Click the stopwatch next to the Source Text property.

❺   Move the Current Time Indicator to a later point in time.

❻   Using the Type tool, highlight the text in the Comp window.

❼   Type some new text.

❽   Repeat steps four through six as many times as you want.

Each time you type new text, After Effects will add a keyframe to the Source Text property. These are hold keyframes, which means the text won't morph from one word (or phrase) to the next. As your comp plays, the text at one keyframe will remain onscreen, as is, until the Current Time Indicator reaches the next keyframe, at which point it will pop to its new look.

In addition to changing wording at keyframe intervals, you can also adjust character and paragraph properties. As long as the Source Text stopwatch is turned on, any adjustments you make will be recorded as a keyframe at the location of the Current Time Indicator.

Note: To quickly highlight text for editing, double-click a Source Text keyframe.

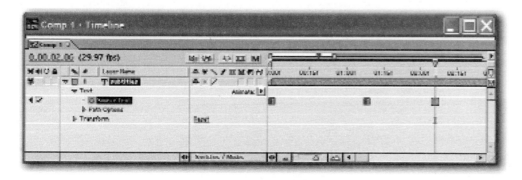

Text on a Path

After Effects can wrap your text around a mask path and even animate the text sliding along the path. Remember that masks can be animated (by keyframing the Mask Shape property) so you can place (or slide) text around a morphing, undulating path.

Create a Text Layer.

❶ Create a Mask path (using the pen tool, pasting from Illustrator or Photoshop, or by using the Layer>Autotrace command). If the mask is closed, set its mode to None (so it doesn't act like a normal mask and hide part of your text layer).

❷ Twirl open the text layer to reveal its adjustable properties.

❸ Twirl open the Path Options property group.

❹ Select the path from the Path property's dropdown menu.

❺ After Effects will instantly wrap the text around the path, and also add some new properties (for animation) in the Path Options property group.

❻ To animate the text sliding along the path, keyframe the First Margin property.

❼ To flip your text to the opposite side of the mask (i.e., outside of a circle instead of inside of a circle), set the Reverse Path property to On.

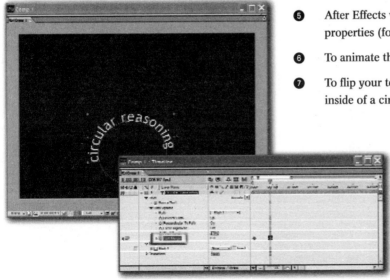

98

Animators, Properties, and Selectors

You can animate text on a text layer, character by character if you want. To do so, you will have to add new items to the Timeline. These items are called Animator Groups, Properties and Selectors.

Properties are the specific aspects you can animate. For instance, if you want each letter in the word cat to, in turn, grow bigger, then smaller (cat, Cat, cat, cat, cat), you need to add a Scale property.

Selectors constrain your property animations to particular characters within a text later. For instance, if you want to animate the scale of only the P's in the word "hippo," you need to add a Selector that isolates them from the rest of the word (hippo).

Properties and Selectors are contained within Animator groups. To animate letters rotating, you add and Animator Group to the text later. Within the Animator Group, you'll find a default Selector, which (by default) selects all of the characters on the layer. You'll also find a default property (in this example, rotation). If you want, you can add additional Properties and Selectors to Animator Groups. You can also add more than one Animator Group to a single text later.

Paint with your Scene

Trying to decide which color to use for your type? Consider using the Eyedropper tool to sample color. In the text color parameter, you can grab an Eyedropper and then pick a color from within your scene. Consider using one of the lighter elements of your scene for white. The color will likely have a small colorcast to it, and that' is a good thing. This persistence of color will help tie the graphic and background together.

Animating Text: Multiple Properties

When you choose an option from the Animate menu in the Timeline (which you can find by twirling open the Text layer), it looks like you're choosing just a property (i.e., Scale or Rotation). In fact, you're adding a whole Animator Group to the Timeline. The group will contain the property you selected. It will also contain a Selector, called Range Selector 1. You can then add additional properties to this group. To test this technique, try the following:

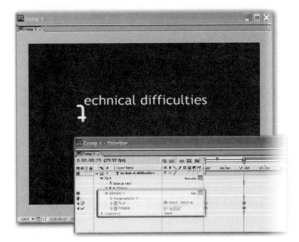

❶ Create a text layer (i.e., the word "hello").

❷ Twirl open the layer in the timeline and choose Scale from the Animate dropdown menu. (After Effects will add a new property group called Animator 1 to the text layer and a new property, Scale, to the group.)

❸ Keyframe the Scale property so that it's 100 percent at 00;00;00;00 and 200 percent at 00;00;01;00. Make sure you animate Scale in the Animator 1 group, not the Transform group. You may want to click the small unlock icon to the left of Scale's width and height values. This will allow you to change just the height value without AE automatically adjusting the width value (or vice versa).

❹ Twirl open the Range Selector 1 property group (this is the default Selector), and decrease the End property until just the first character is selected (if your word is "hello," you'll have to decrease End to about 15 percent.)

❺ If you replay the animation at this point, only the first letter will grow from smaller to bigger. This is because the Selector, Range Selector 1, has selected it (and only it), and the Scale Property has animated it.

❻ Now try adding a second property, like Rotation, by clicking the Add menu in the Timeline, and choosing Property>Rotation.

❼ Keyframe the new Rotation property so that it's zero degrees at 00;00;00;00 and 180 degrees at 00;00;01;00.

As the first character grows, it also rotates. It grows and rotates, because you've added two properties, Scale and Rotation, to the same Animator group (Animator 1). The animation only happens to the first character, because both properties are constrained by the same Selector, Range Selector 1.

Animating Text: Multiple Selectors

If you want to animate changes to multiple, non-contiguous characters of a word (big and small big and small), you'll need to add multiple Selectors. Each Selector will isolate a specific character or group of characters.

Add an Animator Group to your text layer by twirling it open in the Timeline and choosing a property, like Scale, from the Animate menu.

Animate the Scale property, in the Animate 1 group, so that it's 100 percent at 00;00;00;00 and 200 percent at 00;00;01;00.

Range Selector 1 is the Animator Group's default Selector. Twirl it open, and decrease its End property until only the first character is isolated. (It may be easier to do this if the Current Time Indicator is parked a little ways into the animation, so you can clearly see that the first character is scaled bigger than the rest of the characters.)

Add a second Selector by clicking the Add menu in the Timeline and choosing Selector>Range. (After Effects will add a new property group to the Timeline, called Range Selector 2)

❶ Twirl open Range Selector 2 and adjust its Start and End properties until it isolates a middle character in the word.

❷ Add another Selector (Range Selector 3), and adjust its Start property so that it isolates the final letter in the word.

❸ Now, as you watch the animation, the first, middle last characters (and only those characters) will grow. If you want you can animate additional properties, like Rotation or Fill Color, by adding them from the Add menu in the Timeline (Add>Property>Property Name). No matter how many properties you animate, the animations will only affect the first, middle and last characters, because you've isolated those characters with your three Selectors.

Selector Speed Tip I

If you want to animate the middle three letters in the word adobe, highlight them with the Type tool before adding an Animator Group. Then, when you add the group, AE will adjust Range Selector 1's Start and End properties so they isolate just the letters, dob.

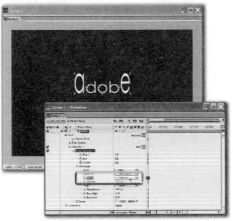

Selector Speed Tip II

If you want to animate the a and e in the word adobe, you don't need to add two Selectors. Instead, highlight the letters dob, then add an Animator Group. AE will automatically isolate dob in Range Selector 1. Twirl open Range Selector 1 in the Timeline, then Twirl open Advanced. From the Mode property dropdown menu, select the Subtract option.

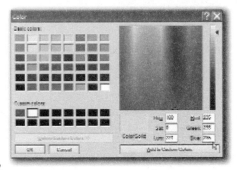

Black is Black and White is White?

It's likely that you will use white and black in your text. Using the standard RGB picker, you'll need to use a value of 235 in order to achieve a video-safe white. For black, you should really use a value of 16. In After ffects 6.5 you can now use the more familiar Adobe Color picker and have greater control over your color selections.

Animating Text: When to Add What

Add additional Properties to the same Animator Group (i.e., Animator 1) when you want the range of characters isolated by that group's Selectors to be animated in some new way. For instance, if you've used the group's Selector to isolate the third character, any properties that you add and animate will only affect the third character. (heLlo)

Add additional Selectors to the same Animator Group when you want to isolate multiple ranges of (non-contiguous) characters. Any properties that you've added to the group will affect all of the characters isolated by the Selectors in that same group. (hEllO)

Add an additional Animator Group (by selecting a new Property from the Animate menu in the Timeline) when you want to animate two properties and have each selector only affect one of those two properties (hEllo). In this case, you'd animate one property in Animator 1 and the other in Animator 2. You should also add multiple Animator Groups if you want to animate the same property for two Selectors, but you want to animate each Selector's range by a different amount. For instance, you might want both the first and last characters of a word to grow larger, but the end to grow larger than the first (hellO). In this case, you'd add choose Scale twice from the Animate menu in the Timeline and use the default Range Selector in Animate 1 to isolate the first character and the default Range Selector in Animate 2 to isolate the last character.

Animating Text: Selector Offsets

The easiest way to animate character-by-character change is by keyframing a Selector's Offset property.

Type the word "hello" in the comp window, using the Type tool.

❶ Twirl open the Text Layer and add an Animator Group by selecting Scale from the Animation menu in the Timeline.

❷ Adjust Scale (in the Animation 1 group, not the Transform group) to 200 percent. You don't need to click Scale's stopwatch.

❸ Twirl open the Range Selector 1 group and decrease the End property until only the "h" is selected.

❹ Make sure the Current Time Indicator is at 00;00;00;00 and turn the on the stopwatch next to the Offset property.

❺ Move the Current Time Indicator to 00;00;01;00 and increase offset to 100 percent

❻ View the animation to see each letter grow and shrink in size, one-by-one. You may want to decrease Offset's value at its start keyframe so that when the animation starts, all of the characters are normal size. (You can decrease Offset to values less than 0 percent).

❼ This tip works just as well if you isolate multiple characters with a Selector. You can animate abcdefghi to abcdefghi to abcdefghi. Increasing the Offset property slides the isolated range from left to right.

 Selector Tip III

When you're trying to isolate specific characters using a Range Selector, you don't need to adjust the Start and End properties in the Timeline. As an alternative, you can drag the Start and End handles in the Comp window. You'll only see the handles if an Animator Group (or a property of that group) is selected in the Timeline. If you have more than one Range Selector in a group, make sure you've selected the specific Selector (in the Timeline) you want to adjust before dragging the handles.

Selector Tip IV

Sometimes it's hard to isolate a specific character or group of characters by adjusting a Selector's Start and End properties. This is because these properties use percentages as their values. What percent is the letter u in the word iguana? You may not be sure, but you probably are sure that u is the third character.

To adjust Start and End by character instead of by percent, twirl open a Range Selector in the Timeline, then twirl open Advanced. Select the Index option from the Units property dropdown menu. You can now set the Start and End properties to specific character numbers.

Note that the first character is numbered zero, not one. So in the word iguana, the i is character zero, the g is character 1 and the u is character two.

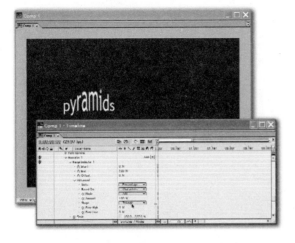

Range Shapes

If you've scaled a range of characters, making them bigger, you've probably noticed that all the characters within the range are the same size: cabbage. You can vary the sizes of the characters within the selection by altering the Shape property (Range Selector>Advanced>Shape). For instance, if you choose the Triangle option, the selected range will look like this: cabbage. You can then adjust the Ease High and Ease Low properties, to make the bigger characters bigger and the smaller characters smaller.

- The Ramp Up and Ramp Down shapes are unique in that they affect characters that aren't isolated by the Selector. Instead, the Start and End properties mark transitions between the isolated and the non-isolated characters. So if you isolate the characters def in the text abcdefghijk and chose the Ramp Up Shape, you'll get this: abcdefghijk.

- The Ramp Down Shape will get you this: abcdefghijk.

- The Shapes alter every property—not just scale.

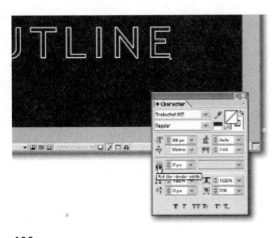

Text Strokes

You can add a stroke (an outline) around character shapes by clicking the Stroke swatch in the Character Palette, and choosing a color. If you want, you can then turn off the fill (so you just see character outlines), by selecting the Fill swatch, then clicking the No Color button in the Character Palette.

To adjust stroke widths, increase or decrease the value to the right of the three-horizontal-lines icon, in the center of the Character Palette. Then, from the unlabeled dropdown to the right of the stroke-width property, choose either to render fills on top of strokes or strokes on top of fills.

Note: what's the difference between the "stroke over fill" option and the "all strokes over all fills" option? The former allows you to make this choice on a character-by-character basis (you could set other characters to "fill over stroke.") The latter is a global setting for the entire text layer. It will override any individual character settings.

Wiggly Selectors

Wiggly Selectors (unlike Range Selectors) aren't used to isolate characters. Instead, they are used to add random animating changes to the characters already isolated by the Range Selectors. The random changes will be made to any Properties you've added to the Animator Group. For instance, if you've added the Scale Property and adjusted it so that its value is 200 percent, the Wiggly Selector will add random Scale changes to the characters as the comp plays. The 200 percent value will now act as a maximum Scale value. So as the animation plays, you'll see changes like this: hello, hello, hello. If you've isolated some characters with a Range Selector, only the isolated characters will wiggle. Try this:

❶ Create a Text Layer and twirl it open in the Timeline.

❷ Add an Animator Group by choosing Scale from the Animation menu in the Timeline. Increase the Scale Property to 200 percent

❸ Click the Add menu button in the Timeline and choose Selector>Wiggly.

If you play the comp now, you'll see the Scale animating. Try twirling open the Wiggly Selector Group and adjusting some of its properties. For instance, you can add more wiggles per second by increasing the Wiggles/Second property value. To wiggle on a word-by-word basis instead of a character-by-character basis, choose Words from the Based On property dropdown menu.

As an alternative to using a Wiggly Selector, try twirling open the *Range* Selector > Advanced properties and setting the Randomize Order property to On. Whereas Wiggly Selectors randomize the amount of scaling (or rotating or whatever), Randomize Order randomizes *which* characters are scaled (or rotated or whatever) from within the Range Selector's boundaries.

Dragging Characters

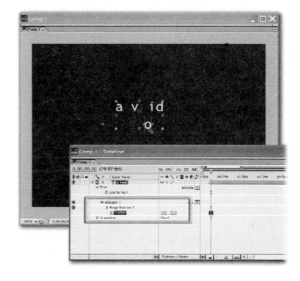

If you've selected Position from the Animate menu, you can adjust the X and Y location of whatever characters are isolated by the Range Selector. You can do this by adjusting the Position property (in the Animator 1 property group, not the Transform property group), or you can drag the isolated characters directly into the Comp window. To do this, you must have the Position property (in the Animator 1 group) selected in the Timeline. Drag characters using the Selection tool, not the Type tool.

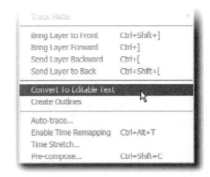

Editing Photoshop Text in AE

If you've imported a Photoshop Text layer into After Effects, you can edit its text without going back over to Photoshop. Select the layer, and choose Layer>Convert to Editable Text from the menu. This will only work with Photoshop Text layers—not flattened or rasterized layers.

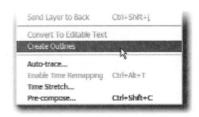

Creating Masks from Text Layers

If you select a Text Layer and choose Layer>Create Outlines from the menu, After Effects will create mask shapes by tracing the contours of the letters on the Text Layer. It will place these masks on a new Solid Layer, which it will add to the Timeline.

Mostly There

Here are some optional tips to fill in holes.

CG Elements tend to look computer-generated. One way to improve your look when mixing lower-thirds and your video is to reduce the graphic's opacity. Try setting your graphics between 85 percent to 95 percent opacity. This will slightly soften the look and improve readability.

Text Expressions

You can add an expression to the Source Text property of a Text Layer by Option (Alt) clicking its stopwatch. If you then change the default expression to "hello" (you must include the quotation marks), the text on the Text layer will change to "hello" (without the quotation marks.

By using text expressions, you can output any property value to the Comp window. This is a useful technique for debugging complex expressions.

Try this: Add a text layer. (It doesn't matter what text you use).

Twirl open the Text Layer in the Timeline as well as its Text and Transform property groups.

Option (Alt) click the stopwatch by the Source Text property.

Change the default expression to:

"X="+

but don't finalize the expression yet.

Grab the Pickwhip tool and use it to click the Text Layer's X Position value.

Now add the following text onto the end of the expression:

+"Y="+

So far, the expression should read "X="+position[0]+"Y="+

Pickwhip the Y Position value and finalize the expression by deselecting the layer or clicking Enter on the numeric keypad. The final expression should read as follows:

"X="+position[0]+"Y="+position[1]

Now try dragging the text layer around in the comp window (or animating it to move it around).

Easy Typer

Apparently the folks at Adobe noticed that a lot of customers were saying awfully nice things about Apple's LiveType. Sure AE's text engine is as powerful (or maybe more) as Apple's, but Apple sure had the usability thing down.

Fortunately AE 6.5 does a shout back and tries to win this battle. You'll find over 250 professionally-designed text animation presets. These can streamline the design process, but don't replace it. Presets can be used as a starting point, and then modified. In fact you can save modified presets or your own creations and build up your library.

❶ You can view the available presets by calling up the Effects & Presets palette.

❷ To apply a text preset, just drag and drop it on top of a text layer in your Timeline or Comp window.

❸ You'll find an extensive (and inspiring gallery) inside the After Effects 6.5 online Help.

Secret Code

Need some random, animating characters? Try this:

❶ Use the Type tool to add some random character on a Type layer.

❷ Twirl open the layer, and from the Animate menu, choose Character Offset.

❸ Turn on the stopwatch next to the Character Offset property.

❹ Move the Current Time Indicator to the end of the Comp.

❺ Scrub the Character Offset property value to a higher (or lower) number.

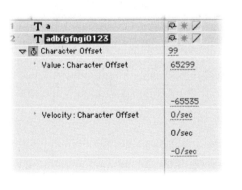

Character Offset will change "abc" to "bcd" to "cde"... To make a code turn into recognizable text, type the text, and then animate Character Offset from some high value down to zero.

For some more fun, try animating Character Offset on text set to a dingbat font (one of those fonts in which the characters are images instead of letters).

Text on a Path

Like many of you, we often start our designs inside Adobe Photoshop. It's a lot easier to do pre-design and visualization with Photoshop's lower overhead. Photoshop has added Text on a Path, and if you work in AE 6.5, this is good news.

❶   Create your text on a path effect inside of Photoshop CS

❷   Save your PSD file

❸   Import as a Composition into After Effects 6.5.

❹   Choose Layer>Convert to Editable Text.

❺   Make any needed edits or animate the path text.

Web Geeks Rejoice!

After Effects offers awesome text animation possibilities. It also offers SWF output… until now, however, text was always rasterized, which increased file size and prevented user scaling. With the release of AE 6.5, text layers can now be exported as vectors when going to SWF.

❶   Choose File>Export>Macromedia Flash (SWF).

❷   Raster filters, Motion Blur and Fill Over Stroke will still go out as rasterized type.

Characters in a Blender

When kerning, tracking or a text effect causes two (or more) characters to overlap, you can control how they blend together.

Twirl open the text layer in the Timeline, and then twirl open Text > More Options > Inter-Character Blending. Choose a blend mode from the dropdown menu.

ON THE SPOT

Key Solutions:
Advanced Keying with Keylight

When Adobe decided to include the Keylight plug-in with After Effects 6, the program's keying capabilities took a huge leap forward. Keylight won an Academy Award for technical excellence, and once you've used it, you'll understand why.

In past versions of After Effects, we achieved professional level keying by using the Color Difference Key plug-in for the bulk of the work and a number of other support plug-ins to help clean up edges and color-correct the final composite. Keylight is a one-stop shop. It can pull a matte, clean up edges, despill and color-correct, all in one interface.

In AE 6, chroma keying is (or should be) the same thing as using the Keylight plug-in, so most of the tips in this chapter relate to Keylight.

Footage Courtesy the Foundry

Shooting for Keying

Are you trying to decide whether to use a blue or green or red or whatever screen? Go with a color that is the opposite of the foreground color. Blue or green backgrounds are often used because there is very little of those colors in human skin. If you were shooting a product that has a lot of blue and green in it though, you might be better off using a red screen.

Make sure that the screen is evenly lit, and that the foreground person or object is far enough away from it (with its own lighting) so that there is minimal color and shadow spilling (and reflecting) between foreground and background.

When lighting the foreground (the object or person that will not be keyed out), try to match the lighting of the replacement background in the final composite. For example, if you're shooting an actor against a blue screen, and you intend to delete the blue and place the actor over a Mars landscape, make sure that the light is shining from the same direction (and with the same color and intensity) as the light shining on the Mars background.

DV or Not DV, That is the Question

The DV format compresses the video image, and this compression introduces color artifacts which may ruin the color in that carefully lit green screen or around the actor's edges. So, if possible, it's best to avoid DV cameras (or any other equipment that adds compression to image data) when shooting for chroma keying.

If you must use DV, you may be able to eliminate some of the artifacts by blurring the image slightly before keying. The Keylight plug-in has a Screen pre-blur parameter that you could use.

Or try this:

❶   Add an adjustment layer above your blue/greenscreen footage.

❷   Add a slight Gaussian blur to the adjustment layer (two to four pixels).

❸   Set the adjustment layer's blend mode to Color.

❹   Then precompose the blue/green screen layer and the adjustment layer.

❺   Proceed with your key.

Keylight: What the...?

What is Keylight? Keylight is The Foundry's powerful chroma-keying plug-in that comes free with the Production Bundle versions of After Effects 6. It won an Academy Award for Technical Excellence, and it's a one-stop shop for keying, spill and color correction.

When you apply Keylight to a layer and choose a color to key out, two things happen: Keylight erases all the pixels that match the key color and it removes traces of that color (spill) from the other pixels. So if you key out green, all green (or near green) pixels will turn invisible, and the rest of the pixels will have their greenness reduced.

Keylight: Where the…?

OK, you've installed AE6, imported a green screen shot, added it to the timeline and chosen Effect>Keying from the menu, only to find that you don't have the Keylight plug-in installed. Unfortunately, this gem of a keyer doesn't install automatically with After Effects. Not to worry, though. Just pop the AE6 installation CD back into your CD drive and find Keylight in its own folder with its own installer. Also included in this folder is a Keylight manual in Adobe Acrobat format. While there, be sure to install the Digital Anarchy 3D Assistants as well.

Keylight: Pick Your Color Wisely

The first thing you should do after applying Keylight is to choose the Screen Color (the color that will be removed and the spill removed). To do this, click the eyedropper by Screen Color, and click a background color in the image.

Note that you can't add to the Screen Color by repeatedly clicking in different parts of the image. Just click once on a pixel that is representative of the general color in the background. If too much background is still visible (or too much is gone), adjust the Screen Strength parameter.

Keylight: You Don't Need a Ph.D.

With nearly 60 parameters, you could easily confuse Keylight with the cockpit controls of a Boeing 747. Not to worry, there are only a few main controls you'll need to adjust. The rest are for fine tuning.

❶ After selecting the color to key out (Screen Color), adjust Screen Strength until all background is gone and foreground is completely visible.

❷ To see the matte Keylight is creating, choose Screen Matte from the View parameter dropdown. (When you're finished looking at the Matte, remember to set the View parameter back to Final Result).

❸ If there's too much spill (too much of the background color in the foreground), increase Despill Bias until you've fixed the problem. You may notice that as you remove more spill, the foreground image starts to become transparent. This is because Despill Bias, which controls spill removal, and Alpha Bias, which controls the transparency of the foreground, are locked together by default. If you uncheck Lock Biases Together, you can despill without knocking out the foreground.

Keylight: Seeing in Black and White

If you switch the View to Status, all pixels will display as black, white or gray. Black pixels are completely transparent. White pixels are completely opaque. Gray pixels are see-through (partially transparent/partially opaque). This view allows you to easily see problems in the matte. In general, it's good to have some gray pixels around the edge of the foreground (so that hairs and other semi-transparent elements can blend into the background), but the background should be solid black and the foreground solid white.

Keylight: Oh Holey Matte

If you twirl open the triangle by Screen Matte, you'll find a slew of controls that will help you fix matte problems. While making adjustments, you may want to toggle back and forth between Screen Matte view and Final Result view.

- Clip Black makes the blacks blacker; Clip White makes the whites whiter. Sometimes when you adjust these controls, you'll find that you'll ruin the edges of your foreground. If you do, use Clip Rollback (a sort of rewind function) to undo a little of the clipping and bring the edges back.

- Screen Despot White removes tiny white specks that are inside the generally black background; Screen Despot Black removes tiny black specks that are inside the generally white foreground.

- Your end goal, as you view the Screen Matte, should be to have an all black background and an all white foreground, with a little bit of gray around the edges. Wispy elements, like smoke, should be gray.

Keylight: Who Was That Masked Man?

To fix holes in the foreground and opaque patches in the background, you can either use the Clip Black and Clip White parameters, or you can use masks–the type of masks you draw with the pen tools. You should only use masks if your foreground is pretty still. If it moves around, you'll have to animate the mask shape (a painful process called rotoscoping).

- If you use masks, make sure you change their blend modes to None in the Timeline, because you don't want the masks to actually act as normal masks; you just want them to be used by the Keylight plug-in.

- To fix holes in the foreground, draw a mask just within the boundaries of the foreground object. Then, assuming this is Mask 1, select Mask 1 for Keylight's Inside Mask parameter.

- You can eliminate opaque areas in the background (rigs or boom mics) by drawing a mask around them, and selecting this mask in Keylight's Outside Mask parameter.

Keylight: View Master

The Screen Matte view doesn't show the results of Inside and Outside Masks. To see them as part of the Matte, choose the Combined Matte View.

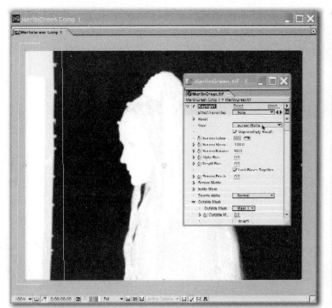 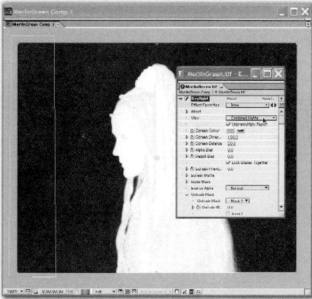

Keylight: Ring Around The Color

In addition to adjusting Saturation, Contrast and Brightness, you can also adjust Hues for both the Edge and the Foreground. You can either adjust hues numerically, by scrubbing the Hue slider (under Color Balancing), or you can twirl open Color Balance Wheel and click anywhere on the wheel to pick a new color. The foreground (or edge) will become tinted with the color you pick.

If you adjust the slider (rather than the color wheel), nothing will happen at first, because the Sat value is set to zero by default, meaning totally desaturated (no color). You'll have to raise the Sat value before you can add a hue tint.

Keylight: Color Me Corrected

After you've knocked out the background, you'll usually need to adjust the foreground colors so that they match the colors of the new background plate. Keylight has two groups of color-adjustment parameters: Foreground Color Correction and Edge Color Correction.

- "Foreground" means the majority (everything except the edge) of the person or object left behind after Keylight has removed the background.

- "Edge" refers to a thin band of pixels around a person or object. Edge pixels often require special treatment because (a) they will usually contain the majority of spill from the knocked out background, and (b) they are the pixels that will be touching the composited pixels in the new background, so they're very important when you're trying to create a believable blend between foreground and background images.

- To adjust how thick a band Keylight "thinks" of as the edge, adjust the Edge Grow parameter while displaying the Color Correction Edges view.

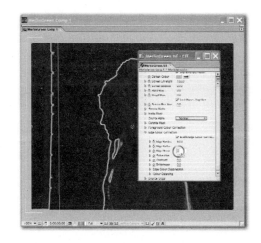

Keylight: Getting a Little Edgy

The Edge Hardness and Edge Softness parameters are not opposites. Edge Hardness controls how much the edge color correction merges into main foreground color correction, whereas Edge Softness blurs the edges.

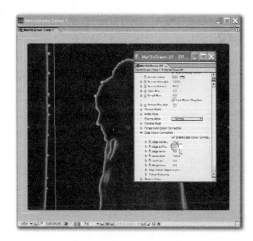

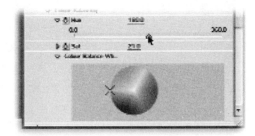

Keylight: 90 Degrees of Separation

Most AE plug-ins view color as existing on a color wheel, with red at the top and cyan at the bottom. You can specify colors on this wheel in degrees: zero = red, 180 degrees = green, and 360 degrees equals red, because on any circle, zero and 360 degrees are in the same spot.

The Hue sliders in Keylight work the same way. Since the default slider value is zero, the default hue is red. If you scrub the slider to 180, the hue will be cyan. (Remember to increase Sat if you want to see Hue having any effect).

If you use the color wheel, note that it's been rotated 90 degrees clockwise. So red is facing East (at 90 degrees, whereas normally it would be North, at 0 degrees).

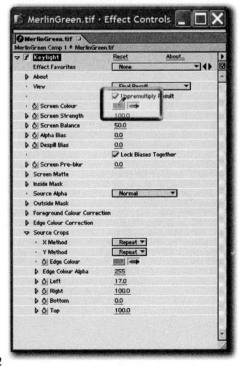

Keylight: What a Load of Crop!

Sometimes you simply want to knock out a whole side of an image–or its top or bottom. For instance, if there's a boom mic showing in the top of the frame, you might want to crop it out.

You can do this right in Keylight, using the Source Crop controls. Twirl open the controls, and scrub the values on Left, Right, Top or Bottom to remove pixels from the screen edges.

When Keylight removes these pixels, it must replace them with something. You can choose what Keylight puts in their places from the X Method and Y Method dropdowns. You can make a different choice about replacing side pixels, which are X Method pixels, from top and bottom pixels, which are Y Method pixels). If you choose, Color, Keylight will replace the cropped pixels with a color of your choice, which you can indicate by adjusting the Edge Color property. If you pick the same color as the Screen Color, Keylight will key out the cropped area.

Try clicking the eyedropper next to Edge Color, then Clicking the small color swatch next to Screen Color.

Don't Scrub So Hard!

When you adjust properties in keying plug-ins, you need an easy hand. Slight, over adjustments can destroy edge detail or tint the image an unrealistic color. But if you hold down the Command key (Control key) while scrubbing any property value, you'll be able to adjust that property in tiny, subtle increments. This trick works for any property value (in the Timeline or in Effect Controls), not just those on keying effects.

Background Radiation

When keying, it's sometimes hard to tell how good a job you've done when you view the keyed layer against its composite background. Detail in the background might hide flaws in the key. You can view the key more accurately by temporarily replacing the background layer with a garishly colored solid. Make the solid color the opposite color from the original screen color. For example, if the original image was shot against a green screen, try laying it over a red solid. Be sure to check the key by moving the playhead to check the key at a few points in time.

The More Mattes the Merrier I

Sometimes one keying effect won't do the trick. For instance, you might need one effect to deal with solid foreground objects and another effect for edge details. If this is the case, use your keying effects to generate grayscale mattes, not color images with missing backgrounds. Then combine all the mattes into a single matte, precompose them, and use the precomp as a track matte for the original color image.

The More Mattes the Merrier II

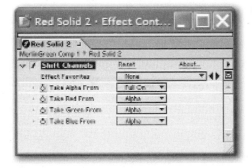

Most keying effects will allow you to output a matte (a grayscale image in which the foreground is white, the background is black, and the edge between foreground and background is gray) instead of a color image with its background missing. For instance, you can leave Keylight's view parameter set to Combined Matte or Color Difference Key's view parameter to Matte Corrected.

If you find an effect without a matte outputter, you can create your own with the Shift Channels effect (in the Channels category). Set Take Alpha From to Full on, and set Take Red From, Take Green From and Take Blue From all to Alpha.

You'll want to save this as an effect favorite called Display Matte.

The More Mattes the Merrier III

Before precomposing all of your matte layers, you can combine them using layer blending modes. Try the screen and multiply modes, which will combine blacks and whites respectively.

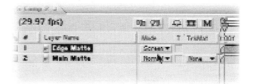

Putting Your Layers in the Blender

If you're trying to knock out a black or white background, there may be a better solution than keying: layer blend modes. If the background is black, try using the Screen mode. This will allow anything lighter from an underlying layer to show through the black. If the background is white, try the Add mode, which will allow anything darker on an underlying layer to show through the white. Experiment with other blend modes until you get the composite you want.

This tip works best when the original image features something really bright–like fireworks–against a black background (or something really dark against a white background).

Getting the Best Key

When using any keyer, you really need to switch your layers to Best Quality. It's also not a bad idea to view the comp window at Full resolution. Keying involves the finest detail of pixel manipulation. While it will slow you down a bit, you'll get much better results and color samples when working with higher quality view settings.

ON THE SPOT

CHAPTER 7

Sounds Good:
Using Audio in your Comps

Audio provides more than 70 percent of the experience when watching a video or movie. If the picture is less than perfect but the audio is clear, people will watch. Conversely, if the audio is poor and the picture is great, they'll get weary of fighting to hear and give up.

After Effects is NOT an audio powerhouse, but it does have some powerful tools to tie your effects into your audio mix. Read on to learn how to get the best sound out of (and into) After Effects.

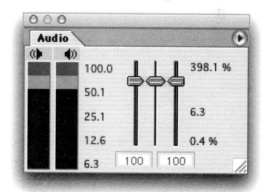

Tap Out the Beat

This is our favorite way to sync keyframes to an audio track. If you can tap your finger to the music, you can achieve better keyframing.

❶ Add a Solid Layer to hold your keyframes by pressing Cmd+Y (Ctrl+Y). Leave this layer selected.

❷ Set your preview area for the segment of audio you'd like to keyframe.

❸ Be certain the Audio button is highlighted in the Time Controls Window.

❹ Start the RAM preview.

❺ To add a Layer Marker, press the Multiply symbol (*) on the numeric keypad. Continue to tape out each audio event you'd like to sync to.

❻ When the Preview is finished, all of the Layer Markers will appear.

❼ To move between markers, use the J and K keys to move left or right respectively.

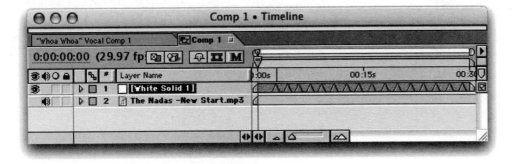

Can You Hear Me?

You know there's audio in your composition. You put it there yourself! Yet every time you RAM preview, there's no audio to be heard. Be sure to check your speaker icon in the Time Controls window. If it's off, it's off. We know this sounds simple, but it's the little things that tick us off when jamming on deadline.

Something Completely Different

Want to animate a Monty Python-style talking head? Sure you do (and you can probably quote at least one third of Monty Python and the Holy Grail.)

❶ Place your audio on one layer, and above it, place the head with its mouth and lower jaw erased.

❷ On the top layer, place the mouth and lower jaw by itself.

❸ Select the mouth/jaw layer and invoke Motion Sketch from the Window menu.

❹ Click the Start Capture button in the Motion Sketch palette.

❺ Gently start to drag the mouth/jaw layer in the Comp window. As soon as you start dragging, the audio will play back. As it plays, drag the mouth up and down in synch with the dialogue. AE will automatically add the keyframes.

❻ When you're done, you can use the Smoother (Window>The Smoother) to reduce the number of keyframes for a tweaked animation.

Original footage courtesy Time Image (www.timeimage.com)

Got Sound?

You can access your Audio controls for a selected Layer by tapping L (for Audio Levels). While there, feel free to click in the timeline just below the Audio Waveform. Your cursor should change to a double-ended arrow, which will allow you to resize the window for larger waveforms.

iTunes

iTunes: Get Converted

Our favorite way to rip, upload, and convert music or Sound Effects from stock music CDs is to use iTunes. We all know music CDs are recorded at a sampling rate of 44.1 kHz. After Effects and most digital formats love to work at a sampling rate of 48kHz. Yes, you can use the lower rate, but your preview times will be slower.

Here's all you need to do.

❶　Open iTunes, which is available for both Mac and PC for free.

❷　Open Preferences under the Edit menu.

❸　Click on the importing icon on the toolbar.

❹　Under Import, select AIFF or WAV encoder.

　　a.　Under setting: select Custom.

　　b.　When another dialog box opens, select a sample rate of 48.000 kHz. Click OK, and OK again.

❺　Now click on the advanced icon on the menu bar.

　　a.　Under iTunes Music Folder, change location to target your desktop. (This will make it real easy to find and move your newly ripped tracks.)

　　b.　Pop in your CD. If you're connected to the Internet, iTunes will go to the CDDB and grab the album name and track names. (Yes, it seem as if most of our library music is listed in the CDDB.) This is great because most of the work is done. Create a Play List of all the tracks you want to rip.

　　c.　Click import, and you are done!

Once you have set up your preferences, just "rip and roll" every time you need to grab a music cut. Fast, easy, elegant, and of course, cool.

If You Need to Edit Audio

If you need to edit audio extensively, do it outside of After Effects, which is not an audio editing program. There are several excellent alternatives available from many manufacturers. A moderate editing audio editing application may run you $99–$299, but its power and speed will be worth it. You don't use Photoshop to edit video do you?

Peak LE

Audio Preview

To hear the audio in your comp, preview it by loading it into RAM. You have several options.

Option 1: Use your RAM preview. Mark the work area off and make sure the speaker icon is highlighted. Click the Preview button to initiate the preview. Using this method, the video track is also previewed so you will have to wait for effects to process. This can be time-consuming and will often result in shorter preview areas, as your RAM will be used up on video effects.

Option 2: You can preview just the audio tracks by pressing the decimal (period) key on the numeric keypad. If you are on a PowerBook, depress the Num Lock key to enable it. Audio will be previewed based on your preview preferences. By default, this is set to 8:00, but you can change this by accessing After Effects>Preferences>Previews (Edit>Preferences>Previews).

Option 3: You can choose to do an audio preview of just the work area. Simply press Option+decimal (Alt+decimal) to preview the entire work area.

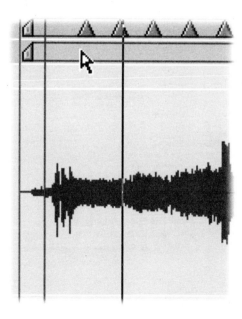

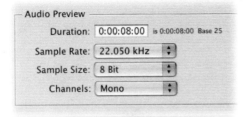

Control the Audio Preview

Want more control over audio previews? Adjust your preferences. The preview settings affect all aspects of audio previews, but have no impact on your renders. To access the audio controls, choose After Effects>Preferences>Previews (Edit>Preferences>Previews). The more you reduce audio overhead, the faster you can preview.

Duration. This setting controls how much audio is previewed when you invoke an audio only preview.

Sample Rate. Higher sample rates are used for professional audio. With that said, you likely do not need to hear 48kHz of audio for a preview. A rate of 22kHz (or even 11kHz) should be more than adequate for preview purposes.

Sample Size. After Effects supports 8-bit and 16-bit audio. While it is important to render all 16 bits, 8 bits is adequate for preview purposes.

Channels. Do you have multiple speakers on your system, or are you using a single built-in speaker? In most cases, mono previews are adequate.

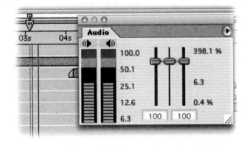

Scrubbing

Want to actually hear the audio while you're dragging through your timeline? Simply hold down the Cmd key (Ctrl) while dragging, and you will hear your audio. While not as good as a full preview, it can help you find your place quickly. You can improve audio scrubbing by turning off the visibility for layers with video or processor intensive effects.

Speed Changes—Hidden Messages

When you were growing up, you might've wondered what all those backward messages were all about on your records, and this might have tempted you to reverse an audio clip. While it may have been cool when you were young, its highly unlikely you want it to happen in your After Effects compositions. If you change the speed or direction of a video clip, its audio file will also change. This may result in the unexpected.

❶ Before changing the speed or direction of a video track that has audio in the comp, you must duplicate the track. Press Cmd+D (Ctrl+D) to duplicate selected tracks.

❷ Turn the visibility icons off on the tracks that have been unaffected by speed changes. These will be your audio only.

❸ To avoid confusion, move your audio only tacks to the bottom of the composition, and lock them to prevent changes in position or visibility.

❹ On tracks that have speed changes applied, disable the audio by clicking on the speaker icon.

Duration	Stretch	
0:00:01:07	50.0%	
0:00:02:15	70.0%	
0:00:03:23	115.0%	
0:00:01:09	90.0%	
0:00:01:03	115.0%	
0:00:04:08	103.0%	
0:00:00:05	30.0%	
0:00:00:07	45.0%	
0:00:00:16	100.0%	

That Music is Hot, Too Hot!

When creating a composition for use with DV material, mix the audio to –12 db. If going to digi-beta, then –18 or –20 db. But don't forget that music and sound effects on Audio CDs are usually mixed to –0db. (Yes we meant to say minus before the zero. That's because music CDs are mixed and compressed so they sound nice and loud in your car; they peak right below Zero db.)

Whenever you use music from a CD, remember to pull its levels down so they hit the appropriate (–12 or –20db) target levels.

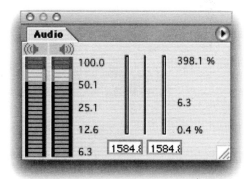

MP3 Sucks (for Pro Audio)

While our MP3 collection is impressive (and legal), it is useless for work in After Effects because MP3 files use heavy compression to reduce file size. When you throw away 90 percent of the information, then try to render out to a new format, you get problems. MP3 files will result in pops and clicks in the audio track. Don't use them for more than a temp track. If you had hopes of using AAC or WMA files, they won't even load.

The best solution is to stick with AIFF or WAV and encode at the settings you are going to use for final file output. You can convert an AAC or MP3 file to a .mov or .aiff file with QuickTime Pro. QuickTime Pro is actually a great program to have and well worth $30. For more information or to download the cross-platform pro player, go to http://www.apple.com/quicktime.

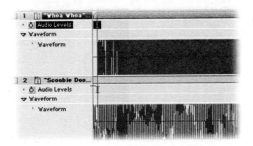

Fast Video=Loud Audio

Changing the velocity of a layer will change the pitch of that layer's audio. As pitch rises, volume will too. If you speed a track up over 200 percent, you will likely get screeching in the audio track. Adjust track volume using Levels. You can find Audio Levels in the Audio property area, or highlight the track and adjust volume with the Audio Palette.

It's Got a Great Beat

After Effects 6 has a new assistant designed to generate audio keyframes. It sounds great, in theory, until you try to use it. The problem is that the Convert Audio to Keyframes Assistant simply translates the entire audio track to new keyframes. Sure, it splits up the channels, and gives you a combo channel, but it only tracks amplitude.

This generates too many keyframes with very little focus. What would you think if we didn't offer an alternate solution? Here's one that involves a little pre- and post-processing.

❶ To focus those keyframes, try the High-Low Pass effect (Pro Only). This filter essentially acts as a dam, and blocks frequencies above or below a specified point. For example a Low Pass filter set to 200 kHz will only allow the lowest drums to pass through. If you don't own Pro, use the inferior Bass & Treble Effect.

❷ To further refine the area of focus, use two High-Low Pass Effects. Apply the Low Pass filter first, allowing only sounds below a certain frequency through. This will clip the top parts of the sound. Then follow up with a High Pass filter set to a frequency lower than the first effect. This will drop all sounds below the set frequency, and enable you to specify a range that only allows vocals through.

❸ Highlight the audio track that you have prepped. Select Animation>Keyframe Assistant>Convert Audio to Keyframes. If you have a long sequence (or a slow machine), it's worthwhile to stretch your legs for a few minutes. This assistant can take a while to run.

❹ If you twirl down the parameters on the new track, you'll discover its generated temporal keyframes (and a lot of them at that). This is a great place to use the Smoother (Window>The Smoother). Select the keyframes in question, and apply smoothness with a tolerance setting between 1.5 and 6 (depending on complexity of keyframes). You now have keyframes that are more useful.

Backwards
Bass & Treble
Delay
Flange & Chorus
High-Low Pass
Modulator
Parametric EQ
Reverb
Stereo Mixer
Tone

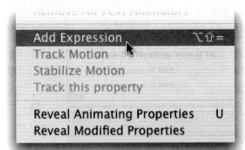

Remove All Text Animators

Add Expression   ⌥⇧=
Track Motion
Stabilize Motion
Track this property

Reveal Animating Properties   U
Reveal Modified Properties

And You Can Dance to It

You've used the keyframe assistant to convert your audio track to keyframes. Now what? The easiest answer (don't be scared) is to write an expression. To get a full grasp of expressions, be sure to look at Chapter 13. Here's a simple expression to tie the scale of a layer to the beat of audio.

❶ Generate audio keyframes, as described in the previous section–It's Got a Great Beat.

❷ Highlight the layer to be animated. Press S for Scale. If it is a Text Layer in AE6, choose Animate>Animate Text>Scale.

❸ Enable an expression by selecting Animate>Add Expression or pressing Option+Shift+= (Alt+Shift+=).

❹ From the Expressions submenu, choose Property > value. Property>Value.

❺ As the text appears to grow, multiply the value by a decimal, such as .25.

❻ Expose the keyframes on the Audio Amplitude Layer. Select the Layer, and press U (for user keyframes).

❼ Use the Pickwhip (looks like the @ symbol) to drag it to the desired keyframes.

❽ Check your expression, which should look like this:
value*.25*thisComp.layer("Audio Amplitude").effect("Left Channel")("Slider").

❾ Preview the work area to test your animation.

Seeing Sound

After Effects offers great effects for creating visual elements from your soundtrack. Audio Spectrum displays the magnitude of frequencies within a user-specified range. Audio Waveform, on the other hand, displays the waveform amplitude.

❶ Create a new solid to hold the effect, or apply it directly to a layer.

❷ You must specify which layer to use for audio. Choose the affected layer, or specify a new audio source from the Audio Layer pull-down menu.

❸ Adjust the several options to create exciting motion graphic elements. Settings of importance include:

- Start Point, End Point: Where the effect occurs.

- Start Frequency, End Frequency. Specifies which area of the music to focus on, and specifies the range in hertz.

- Maximum Height. Turn it up for a more pronounced effect.

- Thickness & Softness. You should be in high quality mode to accurately judge how to set these sliders.

- Hue Interpolation. Introduces variety into colors used.

- Display Options. Choose how to display frequencies; you can use Analog Lines, or Analog Dots.

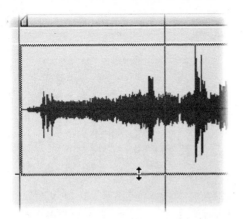

Catching a Wave

Want to see your waveforms in the timeline, Tap LL (think 'Lots of Levels' and not Cool J. You'll be able to 'see' your sound a little better. Want to see more? Simply click on the gray line below the audio waveform and pull down. Size to Taste. Now you can just see where those keyframes are going to go, can't you? If you do want to view your waveform it's best to zoom in on the Timeline. Generating a waveform can be CPU intensive and may even cause AE to quit.

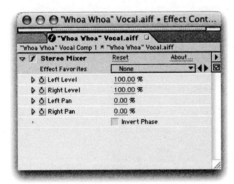

Why Only One Speaker Works

Have you ever had a problem where some (or all) of your sound seems to come from only one speaker? Chances are, that's because you have mono files that are incorrectly interpreted or captured. You may also have received audio that was panned during the edit session. An annoying problem, but easy to fix. Apply the Stereo Mixer Effect (Effect>Audio>Stereo Mixer). You can now correctly pan your audio tracks so the sounds are properly balanced. Conversely, you can use this effect to create stereo panning effects as well for a more "surrounding" experience.

Reel-to-Reel Speed Effects

Just like video footage layer, you can also time remap audio. This can be useful to create sound effects or gradual speed changes in the sound.

❶ Select the audio footage layer in the timeline.

❷ Choose Layer>Enable Time Remapping or press Cmd+Option+T (Ctrl+Alt+T).

❸ You can now add keyframes and adjust their spacing for variable time effects.

Where Did You Go?

By default, After Effects does not include audio in your renders, you must tell AE that you want audio in your rendered project. In the render queue, be sure to check the output module's settings and check the audio box. Remember, most digital sources use a sample rate of 48 kHz by default these days.

Adding Audio After the Render

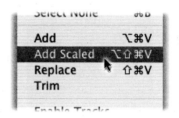

Ever render a file and forget to check the audio render box in your Render Queue? Don't be embarrassed, happens all the time. What's a motion graphic artist on a deadline to do? If you have QuickTime Pro, the fix is easy.

❶ Render out just the audio only track. It should be the same duration as the movie file that needs audio.

❷ Open both files using QuickTime Pro.

❸ In the Audio file, press Cmd+A (Ctrl A) to select all.

❹ Copy the Audio file to your clipboard by pressing Cmd+C (Ctrl+C).

❺ Switch to the new movie and position your playback head at the start of the movie.

❻ Choose Edit Add Scaled (Option+Shift+Cmd+V) (Alt+Shift+Ctrl+V) to add the audio track to the movie.

❼ Choose Save As to save the file. By default, the audio is linked (dependent) so you must keep the audio track around. If you want to create a new clip, choose to make the file self-contained.

ON THE SPOT

Dangerous Curves

Do You Know You're Out of Focus

Can You Direct Me to the Blur?

The Return of the King

Let's All Do the Wave

A-U-T-O-MATIC

Morph Fun for Less

In Living Colorama I

In Living Colorama II: Force Colors

In Living Colorama III: Alpha Blues

In Living Colorama IV: Spot Color

In Living Colorama V: Blending

Colorama: Squash the Bug

Less Signal, More Noise I

More Noise II: Giant Patterns

More Noise III: Layers

More Noise IV: It's a Gray World

It's Fun to Break Things I

It's Fun to Break Things II

Cool Transitions: Gradient Wipe

Cool Transitions: Power Blur

Cool Transitions: Pixilated

Fast Blur, Zoom Zoom

What do I Like More?

Animating a Stroke I

Animating a Stroke II

Scribble

Animating Color to Monochrome

Bad Backlight… Bad

It's So Fast it's Blurry

The (Free) Secret Effects Book

CHAPTER 8

Visual FX:
Effects you'll want

When we first learned After Effects—even after we'd figured out what all the buttons, sliders, doohickies and thingamabobs on the interface did, we were still confused about the effects. Each one seemed like a whole new program.

We got over our fear—slowly—by applying effects to test images, adjusting a single property to see what it did, resetting the effect, and adjusting a second property. We kept doing this until we'd mastered every property of every effect.

At this point, we understood each effect individually, but how to combine them remained a mystery. But we found that after time went by, and we became more and more comfortable using each effect alone, effect mixes started to occur to us naturally. Now they occur to us in our sleep.

In this chapter, we share some of our favorite effect mixes and techniques.

Dangerous Curves

Curves are great tools for color correction—and much easier to use in Photoshop than After Effects. This is because Photoshop's Info Palette displays extra color data while you're adjusting the Curves' filter, information you don't see in AE. Also, in Photoshop, if you have Curves' dialogue window open and Option-click (Alt-click) in your image, Photoshop will display a point on the curve that represents the image pixel you clicked. If you Command-click (Control-click) in the image, Photoshop will plot a point on the curve.

How does this help you in After Effects?

❶ Try exporting a representative frame of your image as a Photoshop file by moving the Current Time Indicator to that frame and choosing Composition>Save Frame As>File.

❷ Then make Curves adjustments to this image in Photoshop (Image>Adjustments>Curves). Before closing out of the Curves dialogue, click Save, and Photoshop will prompt you to save as an ACV file.

❸ In AE, apply the Curves effect (in the Adjust category) to the layer, and, in the Effect Controls Palette, click the Open icon (the folder). Open your ACV file, and AE will use the saved Curves from Photoshop.

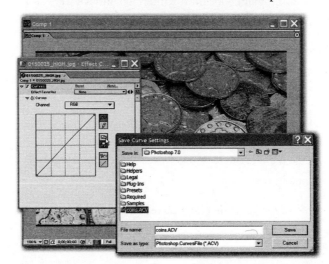

Do You Know You're Out of Focus

For an interesting variation on the Gaussian Blur effect, try Compound Blur (in the Blur and Sharpen category). You apply compound blur to the layer you want to make blurry (or partially blurry), but you need another layer in your timeline as well.

This extra layer should be a grayscale layer. It can be a gradient that you make in Photoshop. You can also make grayscale layers in After Effects, but if you do so, you have to Pre-compose them before using them for the Compound Blur effect.

Regardless of where you make your gradient layer, Compound blur will overlay it on top of the layer you're blurring. (It doesn't literally need to be on top in the Timeline). It will use this overlaid layer as a filter for the blur effect. Wherever the overlay layer is white, the blur will have full effect; wherever it is gray, the blur will have partial effect, and wherever it is black, the blur will have full effect.

Try this cool recipe:

1. Add a movie or still image layer to the comp.

2. Duplicate the layer.

3. Apply the Stylize>Find Edges effect to the dup.

4. Pre-compose the dup, selecting the "Move all attributes" option.

5. Turn the pre-comp's eyeball off.

6. Apply Blur and Sharpen>Compound Blur to the original layer.

7. In the Effect Controls palette, choose the pre-comp for the Blur Layer property.

For variation, open the pre-comp and invert the Find Edges effect. Or, replace the Find Edges effect with the Adjust>Threshold effect.

Can You Direct Me to the Blur?

Try adding the Blur and Sharpen>Directional Blur effect and apply the following expressions to its two properties:

To Direction: wiggle(3, 360)

To Blur Length: wiggle (3, 100)

To adjust the effect, change the numbers inside the parenthesis. The first number (3) is the number of random changes to Direction and Blur per second. The second number set (360 and 100) is the magnitude of change. The number 360 for direction means that the blur can be in any compass direction. The number 100 for Blur Length means that the blur can be a smear of 100 pixels maximum.

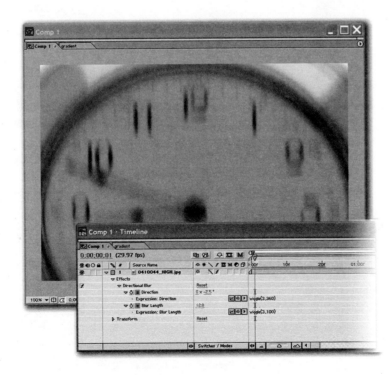

The Return of the King

In the early days of AE there was a great set of plug-ins called Final Effects. Soon came Studio Effects, followed by a new set and a rebirth as Final Effects Complete. The package was picked up by Metacreations and sold for many years. It moved onto become part of the ICEd Effects package and later saw 'life' from Media 100, which sold it with a VERY restrictive license.

Many an AE user lamented about the day when those great plug-ins would come back and be readily available. Well… that day is now! With After Effects 6.5 you'll find those great effects bundled as Cycore FX.

They've been updated and all 61 effects work with multi-processor machines and work with other new AE features. This addition alone is worth four times what the upgrade to After Effects 6.5 costs. When was the last time you got 61 plug-ins in a bundle from Adobe? To find out more about the effects visit Cycore's website (www.cycorefx.com).

Let's All Do the Wave

Need a wavy line? Try this:

❶ Make a solid the width of your comp (i.e. 720 pixels wide) but only 10 or 20 pixels high.

❷ Set the layer quality switch to high.

Then apply the Distort▷Warp effect. Choose Flag for the Warp Style then keyframe Bend changing from -100 to 100 over the course of a second. Option click (Alt click) Bend's stopwatch and add the following expression:

❸ loopOut("cycle", 0)

❹ This will make the wave loop so that it waves over and over again.

❺ Finally, duplicate the effect (not the layer) five or six times to heighten the wave.

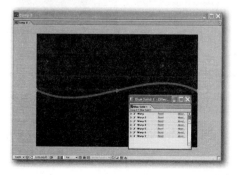

Auto Color
Auto Contrast
Auto Levels
Brightness & Contrast
Channel Mixer
Color Balance
Color Stabilizer
Curves
Hue/Saturation
Levels
Levels (Individual Controls)
Photo Filter
Posterize
Shadow/Highlight
Threshold

A-U-T-O-MATIC

Photoshop users can rejoice—After Effects brings over some timesaving color correction tools from its more stationary sibling. In AE 6.5 you can now access Auto Contrast, Auto Color, Auto Levels. While it's still a good idea to know how to fix exposure problems manually, it's nice to have some options that give you time back.

Morph Fun for Less

If you don't want to buy a third-party morphing plug-in, you can roll your own morph in After Effects using the Distort>Reshape effect.

Say you've got two layers, a handgun and a water faucet, and you want the faucet to morph into the gun.

❶ You'll need to create two masks, one outlining the shape of the faucet and the other outlining the shape of the gun.

❷ Assuming you've drawn the gun mask on the gun layer, copy it to the clipboard and paste it onto the faucet layer, so the faucet layer contains both masks.

❸ Then copy the faucet mask to the clipboard and paste it to the gun layer, so that it also contains both masks. You may want to set your mask blending modes to None, to better see your layers.

❹ Apply the Reshape effect to both layers.

❺ On the faucet layer, choose the faucet mask for the Source Mask and the gun mask for the Destination Mask.

❻ On the gun layer, choose the gun mask for the Source Mask and the faucet mask for the Destination Mask.

❼ On both layers, set the Boundary Mask to None, and keyframe Percent from 0 percent to 100 percent over the course of a few seconds.

❽ Finally, cross-fade one layer into the other by keyframing the top layer's opacity.

In Living Colorama I

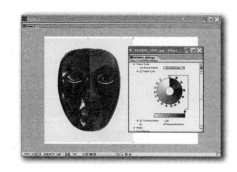

Image Control>Colorama is the most advanced color correction/color enhancement/color effect plug-in that ships with After Effects. It works by stripping all of the original color from the image and applying new colors. You can see the new colors it is applying by twirling open the Output Cycle parameter group.

Anything that was originally black in your image will be mapped to the top of the color wheel, which is red by default. Formerly black things in your image will be red. Then, as the original colors get lighter and lighter, they will be mapped to other colors on the Output Cycle wheel, traveling clockwise around the wheel. White, like black, will also be mapped to red, at the top of the wheel.

- To change colors on the wheel, double click any triangle (color stop) around the wheel.

- To delete a color stop, drag it away from the wheel.

- To add a new color stop, click anywhere on the wheel where there isn't already a color stop.

- Cmd+drag (Ctrl+drag) a color stop to copy it to a new location around the wheel.

Or, choose cool wheel presets from the Use Preset Palette dropdown.

In Living Colorama II: Force Colors

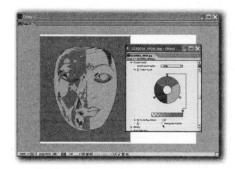

Do you ever need to make sure an image contains certain colors and only those colors? Then Colorama is your baby.

❶ Set the Output Cycle wheel so that the color stops display the colors you want.

❷ Then uncheck Interpolate Palette. Whereas normally Colorama creates gradients that include your color stop color and also blends between them, if you uncheck Interpolate Palette, you'll get only the color stop color.

❸ If you don't need the colors to be 100 percent exact, but you're trying for a poster look, add a slight Gaussian blur to the image.

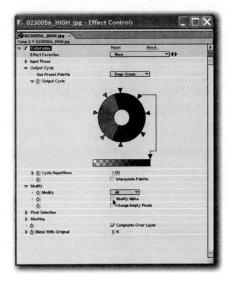

In Living Colorama III: Alpha Blues

It's easy to fall in love with Colorama until you notice it messing up your alpha channel. It does this because it loves to modify colors on any channel–even alpha channels. To stop it from doing this, twirl open the Modify parameter group and uncheck Modify Alpha.

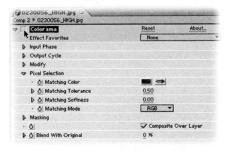

In Living Colorama IV: Spot Color

If you want to change the color of an object in a scene, such as someone's shirt, do so with Colorama.

Twirl open the Pixel Selection parameter group and change Matching Mode to RGB. Use the Eyedropper next to Matching Color to click on the shirt. Only the shirt colors will be modified by the Output Cycle color wheel.

In Living Colorama V: Blending

If you'd like to mix Colorama's changes with the original colors in the image, you can do so in a couple of ways.

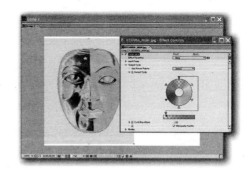

- For instance, you can click on any of the color stops and observe the lines that connect the stop to a checkerboard below the wheel. If you drag the color stop above the checkerboard to the left, that color will get more and more transparent as you drag, allowing the original color to show through.

- You can also scrub the Blend with Original slider, near the bottom of the parameter list, to fade the original image back in.

Colorama: Squash the Bug

Windows users, beware: the version of Colorama that shipped with AE 6.0 is buggy. It will let you choose presets, but other than that, you can't customize the output cycle.

To fix this error, download the Colorama update from Adobe.com, which comes with an updated Radial Blur filter (also buggy in the original release of AE 6.0). After downloading and unzipping the replacement plug-ins, drop them in the folder called Program Files\Adobe\After Effects 6.0\Support Files\Plug-ins\Standard and then restart After Effects.

Mac users, Colorama works fine as is, but you should also visit Adobe.com and pick up the latest patch, which fixes some other errors.

Mac update:
http://www.adobe.com/support/downloads/product.jsp?product=13&platform=Macintosh

PC update:
http://www.adobe.com/support/downloads/product.jsp?product=13&platform=Windows

Less Signal, More Noise I

In AE 5.5, there was a wonderful plug-in called Fractal Noise in the Render category. Alas, in AE 6.0 it's gone. Gone from the Render category, that is. They moved it, and you can now find it by going to Effect>Noise>Fractal Noise.

If you're used to buying interesting background treatments (swirling colors and designs), you might want to put your wallet back in your pocket and introduce yourself to Fractal Noise instead. It's AE's one-stop-shop for all funky patterns and backgrounds.

Sure, it looks like Photoshop's Clouds when you first apply it, but dig a little deeper to mine gold.

- Play with the different effects in the Fractal Type dropdown.

- Adjust brightness and contrast

- Twirl open the Transform properties to find a slew of really cool properties that animate.

- Hint: uncheck Uniform Scaling, and increase the Scale Width category to create water or wood-like textures.

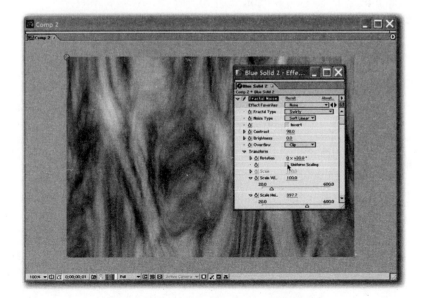

More Noise II: Giant Patterns

The patterns you design with Fractal Noise go on forever in all directions.

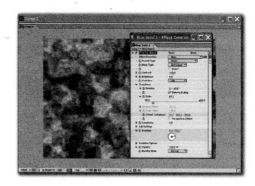

- Try adjusting (or animating) the Offset Turbulence property to roam in the fractal landscape.

- You might also enjoy animating the Evolution property, which will make your funky background morph into other funky backgrounds.

- If you animate Evolution to rotate completely around the circle (and as long as you don't animate any other property), you will create a seamless loop

More Noise III: Layers

Fractal Noise patterns look layered because they are. For each pattern, AE draws multiple fractals (complex patterns) on top of each other.

- You can specify the number of fractals it draws by adjusting the Complexity parameter. Beware of increasing it much higher than the default (six) because this can cause AE to slow to a grinding halt.

- On the other hand, you might like the simpler effects you get by decreasing Complexity.

- The parameters under Sub Settings adjust all layers above the top layer.

- For the ultimate trip, try rotating the sub layers clockwise while rotating the top layer counterclockwise. You can rotate the top layer by adjusting Rotate in the Transform parameter group

More Noise IV: It's a Gray World

Nice pattern, but why so gray? The one thing missing from Fractal Noise is color. To add color to your pattern, you'll have to apply a second effect.

- You could use Adjust>Hue/Saturation (check the Colorize option).

- You could place a solid layer above and set it to Color or Hue mode.

- We suggest using the mighty Colorama effect in the Image Control category. Try applying Colorama's presets to a Fractal Noise pattern until you find a look you like.

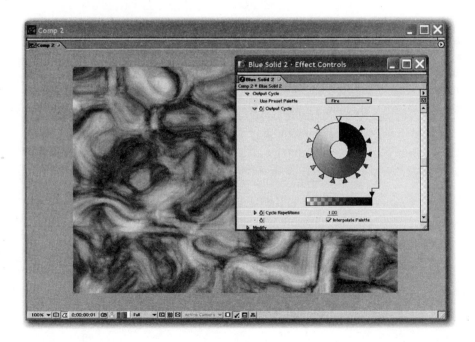

It's Fun to Break Things I

Possibly the most fun effect that ships with AE is Shatter, in the Simulation category. Shatter is one of those effects that animates without you even having to keyframe it. Just apply Shatter, and your layer blows up. Specifically, it shatters into flying bricks. Most people who use this effect never learn how to change the shapes from bricks to anything else. And we're getting darn sick of looking at those bricks, folks.

❶ So please, twirl open Shape and choose a different Pattern (i.e., glass). Or, be more original and create your own shatter shapes.

    a. You can do this in Photoshop or illustrator by drawing a comp size picture. Draw each shatter shape as a filled region. Fill any of these regions with any one of the following colors: red, green, blue, cyan, magenta, yellow, black or white.

    b. Then, import the drawing into AE, drag it into your comp and turn its eyeball off.

    c. In Shatter's parameters, choose Custom for Shape. Finally, select your shape drawing by choosing it from the Custom Shatter Map dropdown.

❷ If you check the White Tiles Fixes option, any shapes you draw as white-filled areas will not shatter, which gives you a way to blow something up and leave specific pieces behind. For example, the layer could shatter, leaving behind a word or logo shape

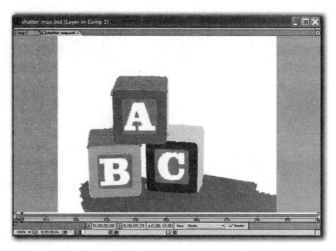

It's Fun to Break Things II

If you've tried to control when Shatter shatters, you may have shattered your computer in frustration. Here's the trick (assuming you want to delay the shatter until two seconds into your comp):

❶ With the Current Time Indicator at the start of the Timeline, turn the stopwatches on for Radius (in the Force 1 parameter category) and Gravity (in the Physics category). Set both properties to zero.

❷ At two seconds, set another Radius keyframe, also at zero, and another Gravity keyframe, also at zero.

❸ Press the Page Down key to move forward one frame and set Radius to its default, .40 and Gravity at its default, 3.00.

Cool Transitions: Gradient Wipe

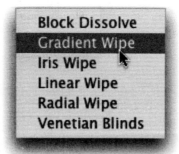

Our favorite transition is the incredible Gradient Wipe. After Effects can use any gradient layer as a "transition map." Create or modify a gradient in Photoshop first. You can combine gradient layers, blend modes, and filters to create an interesting map.

❶   Import the gradient map into After Effects.

❷   Add the gradient to your timeline but leave its visibility off. Make sure the gradient layer is the length of your composition.

❸   Apply the Gradient Wipe (Effect>Transition>Gradient Wipe) to the intended layer.

❹   Define the Gradient Layer source.

❺   Turn up the Transition's softness for a smoother transition.

❻   Start the transition 100 percent complete, and then set a second keyframe to 0 percent where you want the transition to end. When you play back the comp, you'll notice that the light areas on the gradient make certain corresponding pixels on the image layer vanish first; black areas cause other pixels to vanish last; gray pixels cause corresponding image pixels to vanish in the middle of the transition.

Generally, you will need a stack of three layers in your Timeline when applying Gradient Wipe. You'll need the two images (or videos) you're transitioning between, and the gradient layer. It doesn't matter where the gradient layer sits in the stacking order, because you'll be turning its visibility off, but the other two layers should be stacked in order of what you want to see first and what you want to see second (first above second). Apply the gradient wipe to the first image. Don't apply it to the gradient!

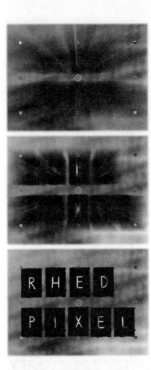

Cool Transitions: Power Blur

The Radial Blur Filter offers several possibilities for interesting transitions, especially on text and logos. The filter is very render-intensive however, so we usually leave the anti-aliasing set to low and apply it for only a short time.

❶ Highlight the layer where you'd like to apply the effect.

❷ Choose Effect>Blur>Radial Blur.

❸ There are two methods to choose from, Radial and Zoom. Most often, we use Zoom.

❹ Keyframe the amount of blur. If you use the slider in the effect window, you can only achieve a blur radius of 118. If you adjust the blur in the timeline, a radius of 1000 is possible.

❺ For a transition, start with a high value, and end at 0. You can also add a small opacity fade into the layer to make the transition smoother.

❻ To improve the effect, try animating the center point of the effect.

Cool Transitions: Pixelated

A frequent effect that does not see much play is the Minimax effect. This effect is really a portal to accessing a Minimium and Maximum command or a combination of the two. The official purpose of the effect is to expand light or dark pixels, often to improve mattes. With that said, After Effects pros routinely use tools in unconventional ways.

❶ Highlight the layer where you'd like to apply the effect.

❷ Choose Effect▷Channel▷Minimax.

❸ You can choose from four methods:

   a. Minimum: Dark areas are expanded.

   b. Maximum: Light areas are expanded.

   c. Minimum Then Maximum: Dark areas are more affected initially.

   d. Maximum Then Minimum: Light areas are more affected initially.

❹ Keyframe the amount of the effect. A starting value of 300–500 is usually sufficient.

❺ The effect generally works best on color channels.

❻ Experiment with the direction menu as well.

The generated effect creates a nice digital stream or pixelization effect.

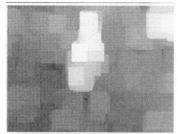

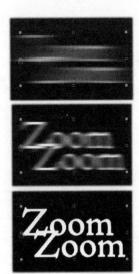

Fast Blur, Zoom Zoom

Tired of the same text effects? Apply a horizontal Fast Blur to your text.

① Select your text layer and Choose Effect>Blur & Sharpen>Fast Blur.

② Make your Blur Dimensions Horizontal.

③ The slider for Blurriness only goes to 127 so click on the numeric value and type 500.

④ Make a keyframe at the beginning of the layer for 500 and make a second keyframe for 0 Blur a couple of seconds later in the timeline.

⑤ Ram preview: "ooh…pretty."

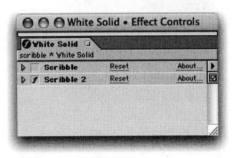

What Do I Like More?

If you spend time setting up and animating Effect properties but want to try a variation, select the Effect in the Effects Palette and Press Cmd+D (Ctrl+D) to duplicate the effect. Turn off your original Effect after pressing the Show Effect Box in the Effects Palette. Change the duplicate effect and toggle between the two to see the difference.

If it's taking a while for AE to render the effect, take a snapshot in the Composition Window and toggle between that and a duplicate effect. This is all non-destructive as you still have the original effect and keyframes.

Animating a Stroke I

Another way to animate wavy lines is to apply the stroke effect to an animated mask shape.

❶ Choose Layer>New>Solid or press Cmd+Y (Ctrl+Y).

❷ Choose the Pen Tool from the Tools Palette and be sure the RotoBezier option is not selected. Draw a wavy mask with at least 3 vertex points in the Composition Window.

❸ Make sure the layer is selected and choose Effect>Render>Stoke.

❹ Choose Mask 1 as the path.

❺ Keyframe the shape of your mask and change it over time.

❻ You can also animate the start or end values of the Stroke Effect.

Lots of smoothly animated, different colored strokes make for great backgrounds.

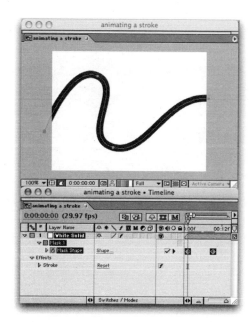

Animating a Stroke II

Appearing tonight...Polka dots!

❶ Choose Layer>New>Solid or press Cmd+Y (Ctrl+Y).

❷ Select the layer and double click on the Ellipse Tool from the Tools Palette. (If you don't see the Ellipse Tool, hold down the Rectangle Tool to reveal the Ellipse Tool beneath).

❸ Select the mask and press Cmd+T (Ctrl+T) to access the Free Transform Points Tool. You may need to make the Ellipse more circular.

❹ Press the Shift+Cmd (Shift+Ctrl) to scale the Ellipse to a smaller size from the center of the layer.

❺ Choose Effect>Render>Stroke. Change the Brush Size to a value larger than 10.

❻ Change the Spacing to 100 percent–voila! Pokka Dots!

❼ Animate the Start or End values and watch your dots appear or disappear.

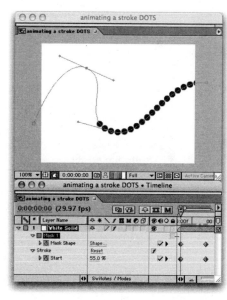

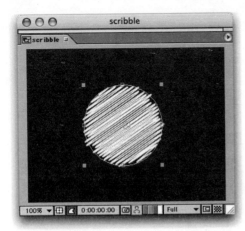

Scribble

A twist on animating a stroke is to use the new Scribble Effect.

① Select a layer with a closed mask.

② Choose Effect>Render>Scribble.

③ Select a Fill Type.

● For varying stroke, increase Path Overlap Variation.

● For more concentrated Scribble, decrease Spacing.

Scribble can be applied to more than one mask and will break up a mask it finds difficult to fill with one line. Check the Fill Paths Sequentially box if you are animating the start or end of a Scribble and want the masks to behave as one. If a layer doesn't have a mask, use Scribble in conjunction with Auto Trace, which generates masks. (Choose Layer>Auto Trace).

Use that Scribble for an alpha! Draw with white and set up the layer as a Luma Track Matte.

Animating Color to Monochrome

Make your own Pleasantville effect by using the Leave Color Effect.

① Select a footage layer on choose Effect>Stylize>Leave Color.

② Use the Eyedropper to choose the color you want to keep, and change the Amount to Decolor to 100 percent.

③ Go through each frame to check to see if you have achieved the effect you want.

④ Use the Eyedropper to select colors at key points to fix discrepancies.

A great way to use this effect is to use it in conjunction with Time Remapping. Apply Time Remapping to a layer and freeze the action for a few seconds. Apply the Leave Color Effect to focus attention on a part of the layer.

You can effectively turn this effect off by increasing the tolerance to 100 percent. Select the keyframes and choose Animation>Toggle Hold Keyframe to turn leave color on for the few seconds the video is frozen.

Bad Backlight... Bad

Have some footage with blown out skies and subjects who are drifting into the Shadows? Adobe has a great solution called Shadow Highlights in After Effects 6.5. Be sure to deselect the Auto Options and then twirl down the More Options portion of the effect controls. This is a powerful and intuitive way to fix troublesome footage.

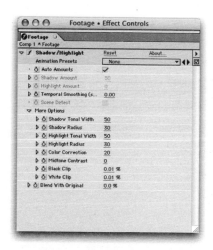

It's So Fast it's Blurry

Since we always needed another Blur Filter, the fine folks at Adobe offer us one more choice in After Effects 6.5. You can now access a Box Blur, which produces an effect similar to a Gaussian Blur. So why choose it? Well, it's a good deal faster and that may be reason enough alone.

The (Free) Secret Effects Book

How did we learn to use all of the effects? Easy, we read the book. You know, the book that explains how every parameter of every effect works.

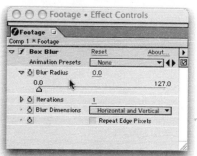

What? You don't know about the book? Well, you own it. It's on your AE installation CD. Just pop it into your hard drive and navigate to the \AE6 Documentation\English folder. The book is an Adobe Acrobat file called help_effects.pdf. We recommend that you print it out, take it to a stationary shop, and pay a couple of bucks to have it bound. It may just prove to be the most valuable AE book you own.

- Among its other virtues, this is the only book that explains, in detail, how to use the five free (awesome) effects you downloaded when you registered your copy of AE at Adobe.com. You did download the free effects, didn't you? If not, reregister AE so you can grab them. You don't want to miss out on the fun of Card Wipe, Card Dance, Foam, Caustics, and Wave World.

- After printing the effects book, you might also want to print the Keylight and 3D Assistants' manuals, which are also on the installation CD.

- If you're missing your install CD, you can download the AE 5.5 version of the effects books, which is almost exactly the same as the AE 6 book. Pick it up here: http://www.adobe.com/products/aftereffects/zip/ae_effects_pdfs.zip.

ON THE SPOT

CHAPTER 9

Blend for Success:

Using Blending Modes for Advanced Results

We want to let you in on a secret... blending modes. Oh sure, you've probably heard of them... but do you use them? Not just twice a year like the fine china... every job, every project, every comp, all the time? Pros live for blending modes... the artistic possibilities are incredible. Blending modes are fast, easy, and powerful... they are also woefully mistreated and underused. Please join our crusade to restore blending modes to their proper place in the After Effects design hierarchy.

A Mode by Any Other Name

Depending upon manufacturer (and even version number), blending modes may go by other names. They may be called layer modes, composite modes, apply modes, or transfer modes. All have the same meaning. It doesn't matter what you call blending modes, just that you use them.

Get to the Modes

Want quick access to your mode switches? To toggle between them, press F4. This shortcut works whether or not the Timeline window is selected. If you'd like to leave the modes out permanently, contextual click on the Timeline columns, and choose Modes.

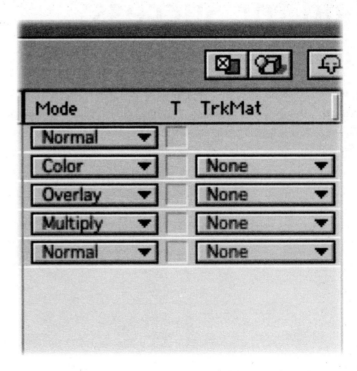

Making Blend Modes Easy

Part of the reason beginners pass on blending modes is that they are hard to use if you don't know which one you want. Find an obscure list; scroll down (forever) only to discover you need to pick a different one. There's a much better way to experiment.

❶ Highlight the layer or layers you want to blend.

❷ Press Shift+= (Shift Plus Equal) to scroll through the list.

❸ To move backward, press Shift+– (Shift Plus Minus) to return to a passed blending mode.

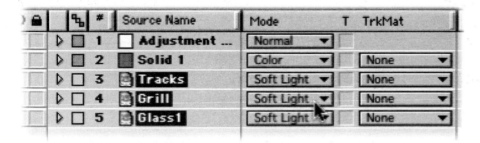

Under Where?

Okay, you're hooked and want to know about modes, but, boy, do those entries in online help make your head hurt. Here's what you need to know about modes.

• The underlying colors are the colors on the layer below that you want to change.

• Layer colors are original colors in the layer where blending modes will be used.

• Resulting colors are what occur when blending mode is applied.

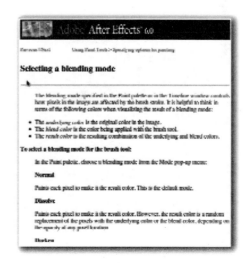

The Bottom of the Comp

Just because you can do something doesn't mean you should. While you can change the mode of the bottom-most layer, you cannot actually blend the bottom layer of a composition. Remember, in order to blend, you must have an underlying layer. If you change the mode for the bottom layer, After Effects ignores the switch.

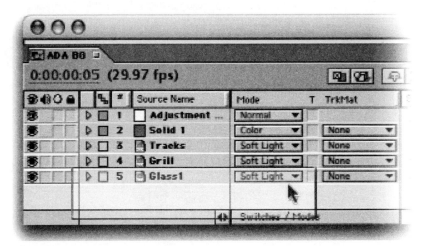

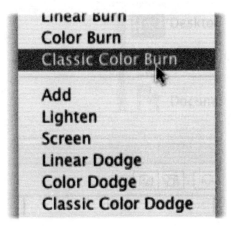

It's a Classic

You'll notice that After Effect's blending mode menu has a few classic modes. These are to preserve compatibility with After Effects 5.0 and earlier projects. The 'house that Photoshop built' changed blending modes in After Effects 5.5 to achieve consistency across product lines. For easier use, avoid classic modes unless needed for an old project.

When Two Alphas Don't Add Up

When compositing two or more objects that have their own alpha channels, you sometimes get a dirty edge. This problem is more visible when the objects have soft edges or are being animated. The solution? Composite layers normally, but be sure to set the top layer(s) to the Alpha Add blending mode. This mode goes a long way in achieving visibly better edges when combining alpha channels.

Luminescent Premul

This obscure mode is there for getting better alpha channels where bright light is involved (such as lens flares or light effects). It will prevent clipping of the brightest color values, thus making a better composite. Feel free to try it when compositing elements created with other software packages or with extremely bright fill areas.

❶ Select the footage in the project window and press Cmd+F (Ctrl+F) to launch the Interpret Footage Command.

❷ Switch the interpretation from premultiplied-alpha to straight alpha.

❸ Select the layer that is to be the composite and switch its mode to Luminescent Premul.

A 'Cheap' Luma Key

Need to quickly knock a color out of your background for compositing. Sure, if it was a color, you could try chroma keying it, but what if it's black or white? Luma key, right? Don't bother. Modes are much faster for a simple luminance key.

• For a white background, set the layer to Multiply.

• For a black background, set the layer to Screen.

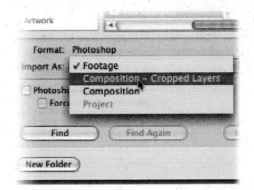

Incoming!

Finally, the left hand knows what the right hand is doing. When you import a Photoshop file as a Comp, all of its blending modes come in properly. Both After Effects and Photoshop made some compromises. Photoshop CS adds the Hard Mix mode, while After Effects modified its Color Burn, Color Dodge, and Difference. The 'old' modes are still there in AE; they are just preceded with the word Classic (in case you weren't feeling old enough already).

3D Blending Modes

Using blending modes with 3D layers is a very different experience. There are SEVERAL new rules to keep in mind when you promote a layer to 3D.

- Use 3D Comp Views to determine actual order in Z-space. The order in the Timeline window does not change.

- When using the Standard 3D rendering plug-in, only those layers behind will be affected by the blending mode

- When using the Advanced 3D rendering plug-in, the mode is applied pixel-by-pixel. In other words intersection is taken into account. This produces more accurate blending.

- Layer Order in the Timeline window still affects track mattes. The layers must still be adjacent, however this may lead to unexpected results. Consider pre-composing the two layers (but don't collapse).

Outbound

So modes work on the way in, but if you want to write a layered PSD file out (Composition>Save Frame As> Photoshop Layers), there are a few modes that are not supported. After Effects will substitute the closest equivalent if you've used the following modes.

Dancing Dissolve	>	Dissolve
Classic Color Burn	>	Color Burn
Add	>	Linear Dodge
Classic Color Dodge	>	Color Dodge
Classic Difference	>	Difference
Stencil Alpha	>	Not supported
Stencil Luma	>	Not supported
Silhouette Alpha	>	Not supported
Silhouette Luma	>	Not supported
Alpha Add	>	Not supported
Luminescent Premul	>	Not supported

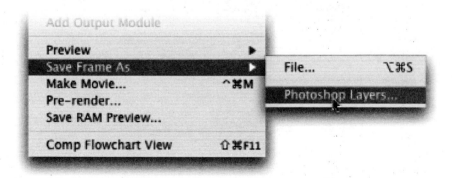

169

Animating Blending Modes

Blending Modes cannot be keyframed in the traditional sense. But hey, keep reading and we'll share a little secret. You can use multiple layers to achieve the effect and those can be keyframed.

1 If you want to transition between multiple blend modes, create a set of footage for each set of modes. In other words, duplicate layer A and B for each mode you want to use.

2 Stack the layers so each Layer A is above Layer B. Repeat for each mode you intend to use.

3 Adjust the mode of each layer A to taste. You will need to turn off visibility icons as you work.

4 Pre-compose the first instance of layer A and B.

5 Repeat for each set of Layers A and B.

6 When you have all of your pre-comps, you can transition between modes. This can be done with simple opacity keyframes. A nicer effect, however, is to use the gradient wipe effect with soft edges.

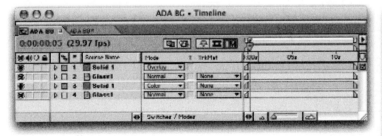

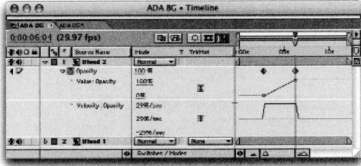

Surveillance Video

Have a dark shot? Don't worry; blending modes can work wonders to lift detail out (without the problems associated with Image Adjustment effects).

❶   Duplicate the dark layer.

❷   Switch the top layer to Add mode.

❸   If the shot is still too dark, continue to duplicate the top layer (in Add mode) until satisfied.

It's a Wash

Need to put some life back into your washed-out video clips? You can use blend modes to increase saturation and contrast. Simply duplicate the washed out layer on the track above itself, and change blending modes. Be sure to experiment with several different modes to get alternative looks. Different source footage may require different modes, but this is a fun way to improve the quality of your footage.

Footage courtesy Time Image (www.timeimage.com).

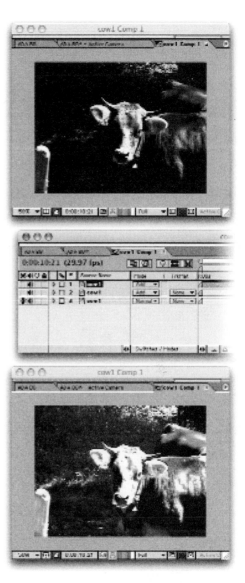

Film Look—Soft Bloom

On several occasions, there has been a crazy notion passed around that Digital Video signals can be somehow manipulated (mangled) into a film-look. While we don't subscribe to this belief, it is quite possible to achieve a nicer look for your flat video images.

The trait that people often are trying to achieve with their "film-look" filters, or recipes, is an increase in Saturation (or intensity of color). This look can be easily accomplished in After Effects.

❶ Select the clip that you'd like to process using the "film-look."

❷ Press Cmd+D (Ctrl+D) to duplicate the shot

❸ With the clone highlighted, apply a Gaussian Blur effect. Crank the filter up between a radius of 15 and 90 pixels. Don't worry if it looks over-done.

❹ Switch to modes and try different blending modes such as Overlay, Soft Light, or Multiply. In fact you may want to try all of the different modes to see which one you like. Depending on your source, you may need to use different modes,

❺ Adjust the opacity of the top clip to taste.

❻ If you plan to animate or move the shot, pre-compose it first.

❼ In After Effects 6.5 be sure to check out the new Add Grain effect to complete the 'look.'

Film Look—Blown-Out

So you want to create a blown-out look and still keep your clip broadcast legal.

Here's a quick way to do it.

❶ Select the clip that you'd like to process using the blown-out look.

❷ Press Cmd+D (Ctrl+D) to duplicate the shot.

❸ With the clone highlighted, apply a Gaussian Blur effect. Crank the filter up to a radius around 25 pixels.

❹ Adjust the opacity of this layer down to about 35 percent. (These numbers will vary depending on your image.)

❺ Apply a Levels Effect (Effect>Adjust>Levels). Lower the Input White slider to about 200 and raise the Gamma to around .75.

❻ Now the fun begins. Set the Blending mode to Add. You will see that your whites are starting to get blown out. Adjust the Opacity of the blended layer to taste.

❼ Pre-compose the two layers together by selecting both and pressing Shift+Cmd+C (Shift+Ctrl+C).

❽ Make the shot broadcast-safe by choosing Effects>Video>Broadcast Colors. Ah ha...a blown-out image that still caps at 100 IRE.

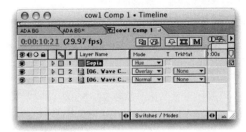

The Power of Duotones

Looking for a cool way to stylize your shot? Make it a duotone, which is a printing technique where one of the inks (usually black) is substituted with another color.

❶ Highlight the shot (or shots) you'd like to stylize.

❷ Add a new solid by choosing Layer>New Solid or pressing Cmd+Y (Ctrl+Y).

❸ Set the solid to Color or Hue mode to tint the footage.

You can also experiment with other blending modes for additional looks.

After Effects Photo Filter Layers

Users of Photoshop CS have a new tool called Photo Filter Adjustment Layers. These try to simulate Photographic Effects such as Warming or Cooling. After Effects 6.5 adds the ability to import Photo Filter Layers from Photoshop, as well as create new ones. If you haven't switched yet, the same technique can easily be accomplished in After Effects using Solids and Blending Modes.

Warming A Shot

To make a shot warmer (or counterbalance blue video), do this:

❶ Create a new solid by pressing Cmd+Y (Ctrl+Y) and pick a less-saturated Orange or Red from the Color Picker.

❷ Set the layer to the Overlay Blending Mode.

❸ Set the Opacity to 30 percent and adjust to taste.

Cooling A Shot

To make a shot warmer (or counterbalance blue video), do this:

❶ Create a new solid by pressing Cmd+Y (Ctrl+Y) and pick a saturated Blue or Turquoise from the Color Picker.

❷ Set the layer to the Soft Light Blending Mode.

❸ Set the Opacity to 40 percent and adjust to taste.

In After Effects 6.5, Photo Filter layers can now be imported from Photoshop or created within After Effects.

More From Your Effects

Everyone wants to get more life from his or her plug-in collection. Now you can–by using adjustment layers and blending modes.

❶ Select the shot that needs processing.

❷ Go to the Layer in Point by pressing the letter I

❸ Add a new Adjustment Layer by choosing Layer>Adjustment Layer

❹ Select the footage shot again and jump to the layer out point by pressing the letter O.

❺ Highlight the adjustment layer and press Option+] (Alt+]) to trim the adjustment layer to match the duration of the shot.

❻ Add any filter you'd like to use (those from the Channel, Image Control, and Stylize categories work well).

❼ Adjust the effect so it is very pronounced.

❽ Cycle through blend modes on the adjustment layer by pressing Shift+= or Shift+- to achieve new looks.

❾ Adjust the Opacity of the adjustment layer to blend back more of the original shot.

❿ If needed, pre-compose the two layers.

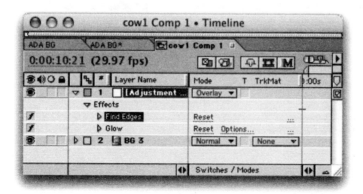

ON THE SPOT

CHAPTER 10

Painting the Town:
Getting more from AE's new paint tools

The Paint Effect is new to AE 6 and we love it. Learn to get more out of the new tool as well Vector Paint effect. Vector Paint has been available, first as a plug-in by Cult Effects for AE 3 and 4 and was then integrated into the AE package in version 5. Learn to harness the power of all the Paint options as a compositing tool and to create eye-catching treatments for footage and stills.

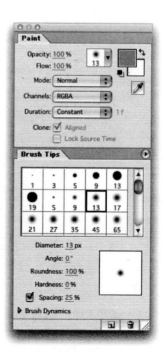

Window Treatments

To use the Brush Tool, you have to launch a layer in the layer window. It will be opened as a tabbed window where your Composition window is.

- To open the Layer Window, double click the layer in the timeline that you want to paint.

- It's a good idea to view the Layer Window and the Composition Window simultaneously by dragging the Layer Window to it's own space on the desktop. Click on the Layer Window tab in the and drag out

You can do this with many other windows and palettes in AE and most Adobe programs.

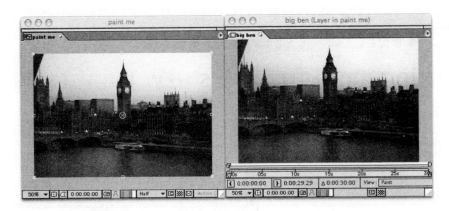

Paint, Clone, and Erase Palettes

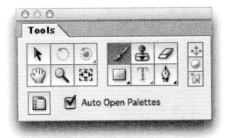

Once you have launched the Layer Window, you can click on the Brush Tool in the Tools Palette. Open Auto Palettes is handy to have checked as it automatically opens the Paint Palette and the Brush Tips Palette. Otherwise you can click the palette icon.

If you prefer to use the keyboard to select tools, press Cmd+B (Crtl+B). Keep pressing Cmd+B (Crtl+B)to toggle between the Paint, Clone, and Erase Tools. If you are using the keyboard shortcuts because you lack monitor real estate, double-clicking on any palette will collapse it and save you room.

Paint Palette Options

Besides the usual options you'd expect to have in a paint palette (like a Color Picker), you can also choose the duration of your stroke and which channel you want to paint on (Alpha, RGB, or RGB+Alpha Channels).

If you are unsure what effect you are looking for, or got excited and started painting before you considered the options (easy to do), you can always modify these options after you've painted. Most of these options can be changed under Stroke Options in the timeline by a quick click.

You can animate the duration by keyframing the Start and End values of a stroke. Notice that if you select Write-On for a stroke that AE places keyframes on the End value as you paint. You can always speed up or slow down a Write-On effect by dragging these keyframes further apart or closer together.

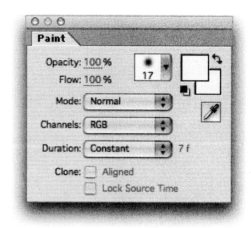

Vertex Mania

Sometimes the masks from Paint Strokes have lots of Vertex Points. It's not a bad idea to smooth the mask. If you have access to Illustrator, this extra step will make you work, but the results are great.

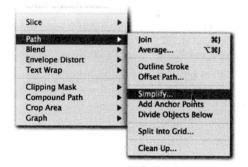

❶ In Illustrator, paste a stroke from AE.

❷ Choose>Object>Path>Simplify.

❸ Choose Preview to see the Simplification, and Show Original to see the original mask. Turn the curve precision up quite high. The goal is to vastly reduce the number of points while retaining the mask shape. Or, close the mask shape, depending on how much smoothing you want.

❹ Click OK

❺ Select and copy the new mask.

❻ In After Effects, paste the simplified Mask into the Mask Shape keyframe.

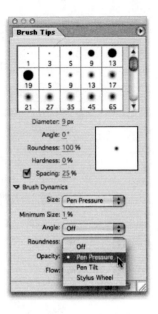

Dynamics

The Paint, Clone, and Erase Brushes have a selection of dynamic properties: size, angle, roundness, opacity, and flow. These can only be used with a pressure-sensitive tablet like those from Wacom.

You can link these dynamics to pen pressure, pen tilt, or a stylus wheel. (Some tablet accessories such as Wacom's Intuos Airbrushes include a stylus wheel). Using Dynamics adds more professional functionality to the Paint Effect and you may want to get a tablet if you don't have one. Other than the ease of drawing with a pen you can vary the size, angle, roundness, opacity, and flow within the same paint stroke.

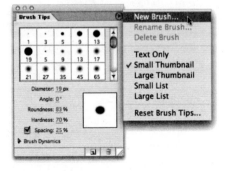

Make Your Own

You can select any of the preset brushes, modify them, and save your new brushes to the library so they always appear in the Brush Tips Palette.

- A fast way to modify a brush from the comp window is to hold the Cmd Key (Ctrl) and drag in or out with your mouse.

- Cmd+Shift+Drag (Crtl+Shift+Drag) changes the size of the brush in bigger increments.

- Releasing the Cmd key (Crtl) while maintaining the drag will edit the hardness of the brush.

After modifying a brush, hit the New Brush Tip Icon on the lower right part of the window or choose New Brush from the Palette Menu. To rename or delete brushes, context-click (control-click or right-click) on a brush

Finer Control, Better Navigation

Feeling dizzy yet? Are you tired of twirling down the triangles to see the paint effects you're applied? It's time for more shortcuts.

- Press PP to see only the Paint, Clone, or Erase strokes.

- Want to change the name of your strokes? Select the stroke and press return (enter), type a new name, press return (enter) again. It's easier to remember what "flower petal 1" refers to than "brush 14".

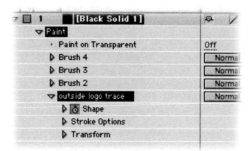

Animating Strokes

Not only are there ten or more properties you can animate under each stroke option, but each stroke also has it's own transform properties separate from the layer transform properties. Wow! Because each stroke is vector have no fear of scaling up a stroke.

Brush strokes (including any keyframes) and individual keyframes can be copied from one layer to another and you can duplicate strokes within a layer.

You can also animate the shape of a stroke by hitting the shape stopwatch for a selected stroke and then going to a different point in time and drawing another paint stroke. (Make sure that stroke is selected after you move in time.

No Alpha? No Worries!

Is your video missing a precious alpha channel? Have no fear, the Paint Effect is here!

- Adding an alpha with paint effects gives you utmost control and you can edit the alpha directly in AE.

- When you paint, choose Alpha in the Paint palette.

- You can change channels after you have painted a stroke if you forgot to choose Alpha.

- White will have no effect (100% opaque), black will be totally transparent, and all other colors will be changed to various shades of transparency depending on their gray value.

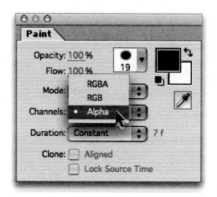

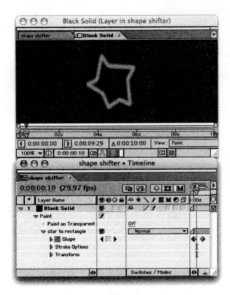

Perfect Strokes

You may prefer to do your pen and drawing work on Adobe Illustrator and the good news is you can copy and paste masks from Illustrator! This only works on a paint stroke but that's OK because you can always make a paint stroke act like an eraser stroke by changing the Channel to Alpha.

❶ Launch the Layer Window (either by doubling clicking or pressing Enter on the numeric keypad)

❷ Select the paint tool, and paint a stroke.

❸ Turn on the stopwatch for Shape and make sure you have a keyframe.

❹ In Illustrator and draw your stroke and copy it by pressing Cmd+C (Ctrl+C)

❺ In AE, make sure your paint stroke is selected and paste the Illustrator mask by pressing Cmd+V (Ctrl+V).

You can paste it over the stroke you painted, or paste it at a different point in time and watch AE interpolate the transformation for you.

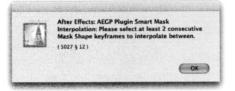

Maybe Not So Perfect After All

There are some limitations to pasting masks as strokes. You don't have options like you do when working with masks.

- You can't change the first vertex, which means you may get strange interpolation even from similar looking shapes.

- Smart Mask Interpolation is not available for Paint Stroke Shape. You can cheat a little though because you can also copy and paste masks from AE into a paint stroke.

- You still may get strange interpolation, and even though these are vector strokes, you can't clean up the intermediary strokes without pasting another shape.

- If you find you want to paste masks as paint strokes a lot you may want to consider just using masks and applying a stroke effect to them.

Frame by Frame I

Rotoscoping is the art of painting directly on frames. Before Vector Paint and Paint Effects, roto was done in AE by animating masks which is still a valid way to work. Some people may find the act of painting a stroke more intuitive though.

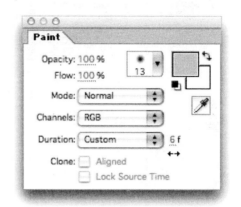

- When rotoscoping with AE remember that the PgDn button will advance one frame, and the PgUp button will go a back a frame.

- You can also advance a custom amount by changing the custom duration in the duration pop-up menu and pressing Cmd+PgDn or Cmd+PgUp (Ctrl+PgDn or Ctrl+PgUp).

The following are some additional tips to keep in mind.

- To zoom in the layer window, press the Period key.

- To zoom out the layer window, press the Comma key.

- Regardless of what tool you're using, holding the space bar will change your tool to the hand tool for fast and easy navigation in the Layer or Composition Windows.

Animated GIF
BMP Sequence
Cineon Sequence
ElectricImage IMAGE
FLC/FLI
Filmstrip
IFF Sequence
JPEG Sequence
MP3
PCX Sequence
PICT Sequence
PNG Sequence
Photoshop Sequence
Pixar Sequence
√ QuickTime Movie
SGI Sequence
TIFF Sequence
Targa Sequence
Windows Media

Frame by Frame II

Paint is pretty great but if it's not working out for you, try exporting a movie as a Filmstrip and painting in Photoshop. A filmstrip opens in Photoshop as a series of frames in a column, with each frame labeled by number, reel name, and timecode.

You can break the filmstrip file into any number of smaller files by setting the work area to a different portion of the composition before rendering each portion.

When editing a filmstrip in Adobe Photoshop, use the following guidelines for best results:

- You can paint on the gray lines dividing the frames of the filmstrip without damaging the file. After Effects will display only the part of each frame that lies within the frame border.

- You can edit the red, green, blue, and alpha channels in the filmstrip file. Use only channel #4 as the alpha channel.

- Do not resize or crop the filmstrip.

- Flatten any layers you add in Adobe Photoshop.

To render, modify, and re-import a filmstrip:

❶ Choose Composition>Make Movie.

❷ In the Render Queue window click the Output Module template

❹ Choose Filmstrip from the Format pop-up menu. Specify the rest of the settings you want and click OK and Render the Filmstrip

❺ Open the Filmstrip in Photoshop and paint on the frames

❻ Save the file

❼ In AE, go to File>Import>File and choose the edited Filmstrip

❽ Drag the Filmstrip to the New Composition button in the Project Window

Treat the Filmstrip like video footage

Playing God

Like the Photoshop Clone Stamp Tool, the AE Clone Stamp Tool works best with small strokes. It's useful to make several samples near the blemish. If your blemish lasts for longer than a frame, or if the area changes color as time progresses, make sure Lock Source Time in the Paint Palette is off.

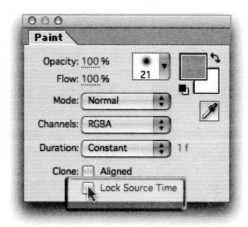

- Lock Source Time will apply your cloned pixels from a single frame to all successive frames

- By unlocking source time, the pixels will be constantly sampled.

- Before cloning, decide which method you want because you can't change this after the fact.

- Aligned cloning will keep your sample point even if you start a new cloning stroke.

- Unchecking the Aligned option will mean that with every new stroke, you will clone the same sample (until you Option-click again to select a new sample).

Cloning Tips

Cloning is mostly used to cover blemishes or for wire removal but can also be used in other ways.

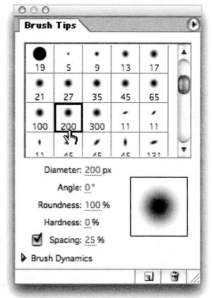

- For example, if you have a part of a video that is not lit properly, you can clone that part with a nice soft brush over itself, and select a blending mode like Add or Screen to bump up that area.

- You can also use Multiply to "burn" an overexposed area.

- Cloning offers great new ways to composite layers, so be sure to play! Instead of using track mattes, you can now do a lot of those effects using by cloning.

Using Vector Paint (Pro Only)

To apply Vector Paint to a layer:

1 In either the Composition or Timeline window, select the layer you want to paint.

2 Choose Effect>Paint>Vector Paint. The Vector Paint effect appears in the Effect Controls window, and the Vector Paint toolbar appears on the left side of the Composition window.

3 In the Effects Control Window, make sure you're happy with the Radius, Opacity, Feather, and Color. But you can change these settings after you paint your strokes.

4 Click the little triangle icon in the upper-left corner of the comp window; a menu will pop up with additional vector paint options. (The triangle icon will only appear if you have the Vector Paint effect selected in the Effect Controls window or Timeline).

5 From this menu, choose Shift Paint Records>Continuously.

6 Make sure your Current Time Indicator is parked at the beginning of the Timeline

7 Paint in the comp window with the Shift key held down. You can press and release the mouse button as much as you'd like, but you must keep the Shift key held down the entire time you're painting.

8 When you're done painting, set Playback Mode to Animate Strokes.

9 If the animation is too slow, move the Current Time Indicator to the point in time when you'd like the animation to be finished, then scrub the Playback Speed property until you see your entire drawing. This will ensure that the entire drawing is finished by that point in time.

Showdown! Paint vs. Vector Paint

With all the fantastic options of AE 6's Paint Effects, you may wonder if you will never use Vector Paint again. But Vector Paint still offers a useful option or two.

Although it's meant for specialized effects, the wiggle effect on a stroke is great for imitating stop motion type.

A benefit is that all the strokes are contained within one effect so any composite option will affect all the strokes simultaneously. For example, if you wanted to animate a drawing painting itself, it's best to use Vector Paint (yes, you can use Paint, but you have to animate each stroke separately).

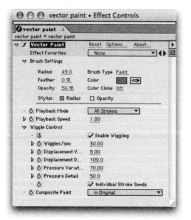

Don't Option Out

There are important settings that you can only access from the Vector Paint options menu.

❶ To open this menu, click the Options button in the Effects Controls palette for Vector Paint. You can also get to options by clicking on the little triangle icon in the upper-left corner of the comp window.

❷ The toolbar appears only when Vector Paint is selected, either in the Effect Controls window or in the Timeline.

❸ If the rulers in the Composition window interfere with your view of the Vector Paint toolbar, choose View>Hide Rulers.

When you use Vector Paint on a layer, you can start over at any time by deleting all strokes or the Vector Paint effect itself. To delete the effect, select Vector Paint in the Effect Controls window and press Delete or Backspace.

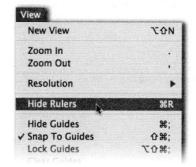

187

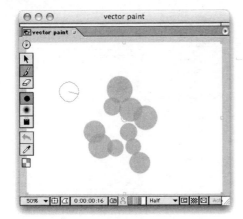

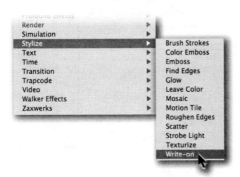

Quick Brush Tips

We often change our minds in the middle of a project. You can quickly set your brush Radius and Feather amounts as you paint:

❶ Press either the Radius or Feather Brushes in the Composition Toolbar.

❷ Press Cmd (Ctrl) and click anywhere in the Composition window.

❸ Then drag in or out to resize the brush.

❹ To change the value by larger increments, hold down Shift as you drag.

❺ The Eyedropper Tool can select a color to paint with from a sampling anywhere on the desktop.

❻ Press the Escape key to cancel the Eyedropper.

The Write-On Effect

If you need an effect that keeps track of the X and Y position of the paintbrush at all times, Write-On is the only effect that does this. This is great for expressions.

❶ Animate a painting with Write-On, add the beam effect to a layer above.

❷ Set the beam layer to high quality and set the beam length to 100 percent.

❸ Place the beam's end point below the bottom of the comp (centered horizontally).

❹ Add an expression to the beam's start point and Pickwhip Write-On's brush position. It will appear as if the beam is painting the Write-On stroke!

Cloning Color

One of the main benefits of working with Vector Paint is that you can clone colors from other layers while you paint. The stroke color is determined by the pixels at the position where you begin to paint.

- The Color Clone affects strokes only while you draw and has no effect on a completed stroke. This is the only Brush Setting you can't apply after drawing. Clicking either the Eyedropper or Color swatch turns off the Color Clone feature.

- Additionally, try Shift-clicking the Color Swatch to open the Set Value dialog box for Opacity (without turning off Color Clone.)

- This works especially well if the layer you are painting is below the layer you are cloning from within the timeline. Drag the layer window out from the comp window tab.

Paint Stroke as Mask

You can copy a mask into a Paint layer, but did you know you could go the other way!? It's awesome.

❶ Draw a closed stroke in either Vector Paint or Paint Effects.

❷ Select the stroke:

a. In Vector Paint use the Selection Tool in the Layer Window to select a stroke.

b. In a Paint Effect layer, press PP to open the Paint Strokes, and select the stroke.

❸ Copy the stroke by pressing Cmd+C (Ctrl+C).

❹ It gets a bit confusing here but click on the pen tool and draw a mask—any kind.

❺ Make a mask shape keyframe and with that keyframe selected, paste (Cmd+V or Ctrl+V) the Stroke as a Mask. Wow!

ON THE SPOT

CHAPTER

Managing Assets:
Importing and Organizing Your Footage

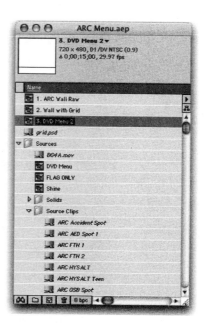

We're often asked the secret to being an After Effects pro. The true power lies in getting off on the right foot. If you have TOTAL control over importing and managing your assets, you'll get fewer surprises and better results. Getting footage into your projects the right way makes all the difference. After all, it's far better to spend your time designing, than it is to search for misplaced files. Let's learn powerful secrets about how to import, organize, interpret, and manage your footage.

Folder Bliss

When After Effects imports a file it creates a path to the file on the hard drive. If you move that file or delete it, AE will prompt you to find it again (that's what all those color bars mean). Even if you tend to not move your assets, the best thing to do is to copy all the files you've used into a folder on your hard drive which is dedicated to the project you're working on.

In that project file you should have folders for stills, video, etc. Organize it in a way that you'll understand months from when you've finished and you want to back-up that folder to remove it from you hard-drive. It's not a bad idea to make copies of the fonts used so that you can open the project up on a different computer.

If you don't want to move a file from the folder you linked to, make a copy and put it in your project folder as well. Copying files may take up more room on your hard-drive but it's worth it to have multiple instances of files as long as you have all the assets you need at the ready. If you are going to DVD or are editing in an NLE, you should keep those project files in the same folder as well.

The Right Profile

After Effects relies mostly on source files created or modified in other programs.

Photoshop can work with files in many Modes or types of color profiles but After Effects, as it was designed for video, has to use RGB files. When you import Illustrator files, After Effects automatically does the conversion but if you try to import a Photoshop file that is not RGB, After Effects will not import it. If you ever get an error that states "After Effects Error: Could not open "…. Unsupported color mode," you need to go back into Photoshop and go to Image>Mode>RGB, save the file, and re-import it.

Be careful when you convert modes, Photoshop will try and flatten the files. Be sure to preserve your layers when converting modes.

A Layer By Any Other Name

Name your layers in Photoshop and Illustrator! Be organized, stay organized. You'd rather animate "small green circle" than anonymous "Layer 43." You can name layers in After Effects but you have to go through each one and remember what's in them. Naming layers properly in the external application also helps After Effects find lost footage faster.

- Choose descriptive and varying names.

- Don't make names too long.

- Avoid using alternate symbols such as { • ^ etc. as there may be cross platform compatibility. It's also a good idea to position layers as you want to find them in AE.

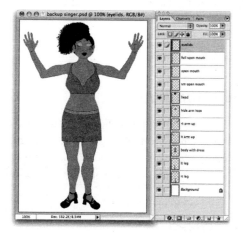

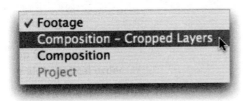

Importing Photoshop and Illustrator Files

After Effects relies heavily on files created by other applications. (AE is a compositing application, not a paint or drawing app after all). You'll find that a majority of the files you use in AE will be Photoshop and Illustrator files.

① In After Effects, choose File>Import>File or press Cmd+I (Ctrl+I). You can also double-click in an empty area of the project window to launch the import dialog box.

② Navigate to the file. Make sure you have chosen to import as Footage, Composition, or Composition Cropped Layers.

③ Double click on the file or select Import. You can Cmd+click (Ctrl+click) to select multiple items in the window.

④ If you select the Footage option, After Effects will prompt you to choose a layer or to merge layers if the file you selected contains layers. If you have a layered file, but only need the composite image, choose merged. The merged files load and render faster.

Over the Border

Have you applied a great effect only to have it chopped off at the edge? Certain effects cannot extend beyond the borders of an image, one workaround is to import the files as a Composition and choose to NOT crop the layers. But chances are you've already imported and animated, so here's another way:

① Select the footage item.

② Choose Layer>Pre-Compose or press Shift+Cmd+C (Shift+Ctrl+C).

③ Choose to Leave All Attributes behind.

④ Click the Collapse Transformations switch to extend allow the effect past the edge of the border.

Mobile Style

Photoshop Layer Styles (formerly Layer Effects) do not like to travel. This is a common problem as there is not a single application out there that correctly interprets layer styles outside of Photoshop.

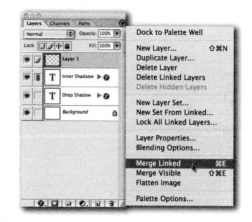

In order to import successfully, you need to flatten them. Using a technique called Targeted Flattening, we can create a merged layer and preserve an editable layer within the same document. This gives you the best of both worlds, proper imports, and room for future revisions.

❶ Save your document under a different name by using File>Save As. This is an extra precaution against accidentally deleting your work. (We usually rename it Document Name for AE.psd)

❷ Create a new (empty) layer and link it to the stylized layer that needs processing.

❸ Leave the empty layer highlighted. While holding down the Option key (Alt key), choose Merge Linked from the Layers Palette submenu. This merges the layers to the target layer, but leaves the originals behind.

❹ You should have a flattened copy on the target layer. Rename this flattened layer so you can easily locate it later. We recommend including the words FLAT in your layer name for ease of use.

❺ Repeat for all layers and save your work. This method will produce a layered document, which will import properly.

Parent Layer Styles

If you import a Photoshop file as a composition and have a layer with a drop shadow or Outer glow (or even layer styles which become effect comps), parent the effect comps or effect layers to the source layer. This way if you move your source layer, the effects will follow.

Think Ahead

Consider the following tips when preparing files to import into After Effects.

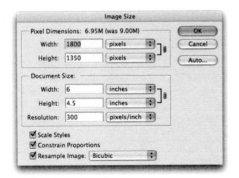

- Make sure your file is the right resolution. If you are going to pan over or zoom in on a photograph, make sure your photo has at least 3x the resolution (total pixel dimensions) of your composition.

- Optimize files. Don't use huge bitmap files if you can avoid it. Crop unwanted information. The maximum resolution you can use in After Effects is 30,000x30,000 pixels (huge) but AE will start to slow down working with several large Photoshop files.

- Save the files with the correct extension. This is especially important if you will be working cross-platform. Refrain from using characters (*&^%) and if you want to separate words, use an underscore _.

- Avoid using very thin lines for images or text because they will flicker on broadcast video. If you must use a thin line, add a slight Gaussian or Motion blur so it displays on both fields.

PS Alpha Channel (1-Layer graphic)

If you choose to import a single layer graphic, you may want to embed an alpha channel. An alpha channel contains the transparency of a document saved as the fourth channel in an RGB image. Here's the fastest way to create an alpha channel in Photoshop for a single layer document.

① A perfect alpha channel starts with an active selection loaded. To load a layer, Cmd+click (Ctrl+click) on the layer's icon in the Layers palette until you see the marching ants. NOTE: If you have a layer style applied, you must flatten the layer style by merging it with a new empty layer.

② Switch to the Channels palette and click on the Save Selection as Channel icon or go to Select>Save Selection>Operation New Channel.

③ Choose File>Save to save your native .psd file. Then pick File>Save As, and choose to save a PICT or TARGA file. Make sure the Alpha Channels box is selected.

PS Alpha Channel (Multiple Layers)

If you have a multi-layered Photoshop document, things are a little trickier. But creating an alpha channel is still an essential part of getting clean keying of graphics.

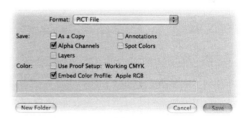

① Turn off the Visibility icon for all layers that are not part of the graphic you want to key.

② Create a new layer and highlight it. Hold down the Option key (Alt) and choose Merge Visible from the Layers palette submenu. A new layer is created from the existing layers.

③ Cmd+Click (Ctrl+Click) on the layer's thumbnail icon to make an active selection. Then turn the visibility icon off for the merged copy.

④ Switch to the Channels palette and click on the Save Selection as Channel icon.

⑤ Save your file as a PICT or TARGA with Alpha Channel using the previously described method.

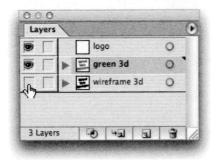

Peek-a-Boo

If you are going to merge layers in an Illustrator or Photoshop file on import into AE, make sure the visibility for all the layers are on before you save the file in PS or AI. Layers that are not visible will be ignored when merging.

If you import as a composition, then non-visible layers will import with their visibility icon turned off.

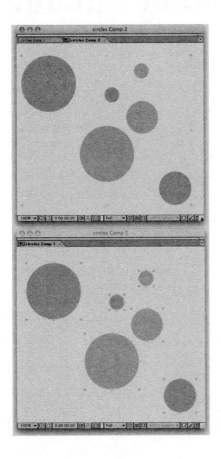

To Crop or Not to Crop?

New to AE 6 is the ability to distinguish when importing a composition as cropped layers or a composition. Previous versions always chose to crop a layer based on its content's boundaries.

- Importing with cropped layers is useful if you will be rotating, scaling, or animating from the anchor point of a layer.

- Cropped layers place the anchor point in the center of the information of that layer. As long as your layer has equal parameters, you're golden.

- You can always move your anchor point though so don't fret. Select the layer, choose the pan behind tool from the tools palette, and click on the anchor point to move it. This works from the composition window or layer window.

- Import as a composition if you want the layer's content to have identical dimensions and anchor points.

- Import as a composition if the filters you are using tend to get 'chopped' at image boundaries. Some older effects and third-party filters cannot draw beyond an object's boundaries.

Merge Me Seymour

If you import a Photoshop file that has layers with styles, the styles will import as nested compositions called Layer Effects Comps.

The good news:

- You can animate some layer styles without a problem.

The bad news:

- Some layer styles are unsupported.

- If you change the text in AE, the styles will not update.

- All the Layer Effects Comps have the same name on import and it is time consuming to figure out which effects comps apply to what layer.

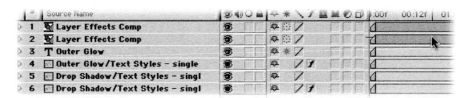

Remember Me?

If you want different footage items to use with the same Interpret Footage settings (such as Frame Rate or Looping), copy settings from one item and apply them to others.

To copy and paste Interpret Footage settings:

❶ In the Project window, select the item whose footage interpretations you want to apply. Choose File>Interpret Footage>Remember Interpretation or select the file or footage item, and click Cmd+Option+C (Ctrl+Alt+C).

❷ Select one or more footage items.

❸ Choose File>Interpret Footage>Apply Interpretation, or select the layer or footage item and press Cmd+Option+V (Ctrl+Alt+V). After Effects applies the footage interpretation options to the selected items.

Designing on a Deadline I

On a tight deadline (uh… yeah)? Missing footage but need to get started? Whatever the reason for speed, use a placeholder or proxy to increase productivity.

Use placeholders when you don't have access to the file you want to animate. For best results, set the placeholder to the same size, duration, and frame rate as the actual footage.

To use a placeholder:

- Choose File>Import>Placeholder or File>Replace Footage>Placeholder.

- In the New Placeholder dialog box, specify the placeholder's name, size, frame rate, and duration, then click OK.

To replace a placeholder with the actual footage:

- In the Project window, double-click the placeholder you want to replace, or choose File>Replace Footage>File or press Cmd+H (Ctrl+H).

- Locate and select the actual footage, then click Import (Mac OS) or OK (Windows). Effects, masks, and properties applied to the placeholder are applied to the actual footage when you perform the replacement.

Designing on a Deadline II

Proxies are lower-resolution or still versions of existing footage. You must have a footage item available to use a proxy.

For best results, set a proxy so it has the same aspect ratio as the actual footage item. For example, if the actual footage item is a 720x540-pixel movie, create and use a file with 3:4 pixel aspect ratio (320x240 or 180x135).

To locate and use a proxy, in the Project window, select a footage item.

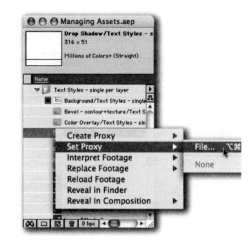

❶ Choose File Set Proxy>File or select a file in the project window and hit Cmd+Option+P (Ctrl+Alt+P). You can also Context Click (Right Click) on the selected footage.

❷ In the Set Proxy File dialog box, locate and select the file you want to use as the proxy, and click Import (Mac OS) or Open (Windows).

❸ To toggle between using the original footage and its proxy, in the Project window, click the proxy indicator to the left of the footage name.

To stop using a proxy, in the Project window, select the original footage item and Choose File>Set Proxy>None.

Proxy Moxie

You can render a movie without replacing proxies, or choose to replace during a render. To test motion in a composition with high resolution layers, keep your proxies to speed up a render.

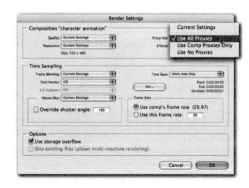

❶ Choose a composition where proxies are used.

❷ Go to Composition>Make Movie or press Cmd+M (Ctrl+M).

❸ In the Render Settings>Proxy Use and choose to use all proxies.

Illustrator Ease

Illustrator is fundamentally a page design program and will default to creating letter size pages with inches as units. Illustrator is versatile though, and you can choose to work at any size. Let's assume you are designing at 720x540 (which is equivalent to 720x486 in non-square pixels):

❶ In Illustrator, go to File>New or press Cmd+N (Ctrl+N).

❷ In the New Document Dialog Box, change the units to Pixels.

❸ Change the Width to 720 and the Height to 540.

❹ Choose RGB for the color profile. After Effects can import CMYK Illustrator files. It applies a CMYK to RGB conversion on import but this may result in a subtle shift in color. You should design in RGB to avoid color shift.

After Effects is versatile too and could work with a letter-sized file but things like anchor points will be all out of whack. Its just good practice to work with your composition and purpose in mind.

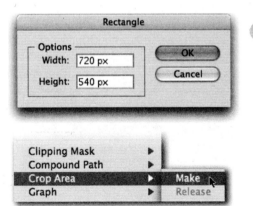

Illustrator: Holy Crop Marks!

After Effects tends to crop Illustrator files to the size of the largest layer. Creating crop marks ultimately save you time in the long-run. In a new 720x540 Illustrator file:

❶ Select the rectangle tool.

❷ Double click in the work area.

❸ You will be prompted to enter values for the size of a new rectangle. Type 720 for width and 540 for height (720x534 if you are designing for DV or DVD).

❹ A new rectangle is created. It helps if it is a bright color, like red. To change it's color click on a swatch.

❺ Position the rectangle perfectly over the 720x540 artboard. Use the arrow keys to nudge. Go to Object>Crop Area>Make.

❻ Save the file and continue to design.

Templates

Illustrator defaults to the settings last entered in the dialog box when you create a new file. This is useful, but invest a little time to make templates for yourself.

In each template create a rectangle and make crop marks. Place guides at 10 percent and 20 percent for Action safe and Title safe areas.

In Illustrator CS you can save a file as a template automatically.

Save As...	⇧⌘S
Save a Copy...	⌥⌘S
Save as Template...	
Save for Web...	⌥⇧⌘S
Save a Version...	
Revert	F12

- In Illustrator CS, go to File>Save As Template.

- Navigate to your Applications folder and select the AI program folder. Inside you'll find a templates folder, open it. Create a New Folder and call it Video.

- Name the file with it's pixel dimensions and make sure it has the .ait extension. Save it to the Video folder.

- To use a template, go to File>New from Template>Video Folder and choose one of your templates. You can also jump right to the templates folder by pressing Shift+Cmd+N (Shift+Ctrl+N).

It's not quite as easy in Illustrator 10 (or earlier) as you have to manage your own templates.

- Create a folder on your hard-drive for Illustrator Video Templates.

- In Illustrator, go to File>Save and navigate to your Illustrator templates folder

- Save the file with dimensions in the title.

- When you need to use the template open it, start designing, and go to File>Save As. Rename it and save it to your project folder.

Ode To the Vector

You can't scale a bitmap much over 100 percent without noticing degradation but Illustrator files are vector and can be scaled infinitely (or until the RAM runs out). When you scale a layer that originated in Illustrator more than 100 percent, use Continuous Rasterization.

To continuously rasterize an Illustrator file, do the following.

❶ Select the layer containing the Illustrator file in the Timeline window.

❷ Click the Collapse Transformations/Continuously Rasterize switch so that the On icon appears for that layer. (It looks like a Sun).

Notes about continuous rasterization

- When you continuously rasterize a layer, the default rendering order for the layer changes. Applying an effect to a continuously rasterized layer may be different than when you apply the effect to a non-rasterized layer.

- Continuous rasterization will not affect Illustrator layers with raster Illustrator effects applied. In Illustrator, notice the line that separates the effects and filters into top and bottom? The effects and filters above the line are Vector, and those below the line are Raster. None of the raster effects will be helped by continuous rasterization and will pixelate like any bitmap layer if you scale them more than 100 percent.

- You can't paint interactively on a continuously rasterized layer. You can apply a paint effect by copying and pasting or using the Favorites menu but the results are not great. When you Continuously Rasterize a layer, its Layer window closes and won't open until you turn Continuously Rasterize off.

- Whether or not you choose to Continuously Rasterize, After Effects anti-aliases the art if you view and render a composition using Best Quality.

How Did I Do That Again?

Need to open a recent project to see how you achieved an effect? You don't need to close your current project. Go to File>Import or press Cmd+I (Ctrl+I) and import that project.

This works best if you've been organized and put all your source files in the same folder as your project file. If After Effects can't find a file, it substitutes a placeholder.

To re-link or replace a reference:

❶ Select the placeholder or footage file in the Project window, and choose File>Replace Footage>File or double-click on the placeholder.

❷ In the Replace Footage File dialog box, locate and select the footage file you want to use.

So Many Files To Import

Have a folder of files ready to import into AE?

- In After Effects go to File Import>File>Select a folder. Choose Import folder. Alternatively you could Option Click (Alt-click) and drag this folder from the hard-drive into the AE project window. But be sure to click on the folder first without the option key held down, otherwise the Mac OS will minimize After Effects.

- If you don't hold down the Option key when you drag over a folder, After Effects will treat the folder as an image sequence.

- If you import files this way it's best to not use layered files unless you want to merge layers. AE will prompt you to choose a layer or merge layers if it encounters layered files. To import more then one layer from a file, import it separately as a composition.

- To import multiple files go to File>Import>Multiple Files or hit Cmd+Option+I (Ctrl+Alt+I). You can choose to import them as footage or compositions. When you are done importing, press done in the import dialog box.

Internal Folder Bliss

It's a good idea to stay organized in the AE project window as well as your hard-drive. Make folders for your artwork, Photoshop files, and imported video. It helps to stay consistent from project to project so you know what to expect from yourself.

To import directly into a folder, select a folder in the project window and import a file in any of the following ways:

- Hit Cmd+I (Ctrl+I).

- Go to File>Import>File.

- Double-click anywhere in the project window.

Any file you import will reside in the folder you selected pre-import. You can move from file to file in the project window by using the arrow keys.

To add folders to your project window click the new folder button at the bottom of the project window or press Cmd+Option+Shift+N (Ctrl+Alt+Shift+N).

To delete files and folders from the project window, select them and hit delete. To avoid the warning, select the files and hit Cmd+Delete (Ctrl+Delete).

Oops, Wrong Footage!

Need to do a last minute substitution?

1. Select the footage you want to replace in the timeline.

2. Then select the file you'd rather use in the project window.

3. Hold the Option (Alt) key and drag the preferred file onto the selected file in the timeline. Alternatively select the files and hit Cmd+Option+/ (Ctrl+Alt+/).

4. The files will swap out but any effects, masks, and keyframes will be applied to the preferred layer.

This is an excellent way to create multiple versions of a composition. To add footage to a composition, select and drag a file from the project window, or select the file in the project window and hit Command+/.

Solid State

They're alive! After Effects 6 solids seem so smart. They name themselves and place themselves neatly into the Solids folder. Sometimes though, as cool as it is for a layer to know exactly what shade of green it is, you need a more descriptive name. Create a new solid: Layer>New>Solid or Cmd+Y (Ctrl+Y) and name the layer in the Solid Settings Dialog Box. You can call up this box again by choosing Layer>Solid Settings or Cmd+Shift+Y (Ctrl+Shift+Y).

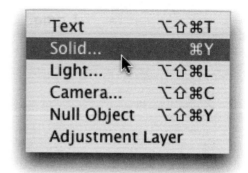

- Solids can be reused so there is no need to keep creating them. You can copy and paste solids or adjustment layers within a comp and from comp to comp.

- Solids can be used like instances. Changing one can change all duplicates of the solid. This is useful if you use a colored solid with a blending mode to create a color cast in several compositions and your client wants you to change the hue.

- Not creating a ton of solids and adjustment layers also keeps your project file size down.

- Under AE 6.5, solids can also be continuously rasterized. This will enable the edges to hold up better when you've scaled or positioned a solid.

    - This is useful when using masks

    - Be sure to click the Collapse Transformations/Continuously Rasterize switch so that it is on.

Bad Alpha?

If the alpha channel on a layer isn't looking right, select the layer in the project window and Context Click or hit Cmd+F (Ctrl+F) to see the footage's interpretation.

- If After Effects guessed that your alpha was premultiplied, trying using a different color matte. If that doesn't help, change the interpretation to straight. Do you still have a questionable alpha channel? Get creative. Try using the paint effects set to alpha, then use auto trace, or draw a mask.

- If you don't want an alpha select None. This will make it easier to apply a track matte or to draw a mask to the layer.

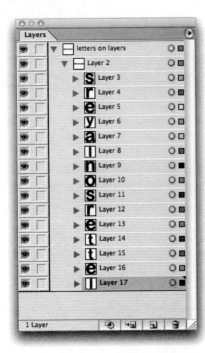

Need Your Letters on Separate Layers?

Set your type in Illustrator and position it.

1 Select the type and choose Type>Create Outlines.

2 Select the layer in the layers palette and toggle the triangle by the layer name.

3 Select the group layer and go to the layer palette menu.

4 Choose Release to Layers (Sequence).

5 In the layers palette, select the layers of your text (shift click to select more than one layer) and drag them out of the group.

6 Delete the empty layer by dragging it to the trash.

7 Double click on each layer and name them the letter they contain.

8 Import as a composition (cropped layers) into AE and animate.

Layer Stretch

Need to make your footage duration fit your composition? You can let After Effects figure out how much stretch you really need. These two techniques are useful when you need to lengthen or shorten a shot.

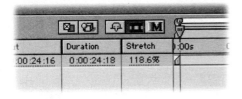

Method 1

To maintain your layer's out-point, you can stretch toward the beginning of the Composition. Press Cmd+Shift+Comma (Ctrl+Shift+Comma) to Time Stretch the In-point of a Layer.

Method 2

To maintain your layer's in-point, you can stretch toward the end of the Composition. Press Cmd+Option+Comma (Ctrl+Alt+Comma) to Time Stretch the Out Point of a Layer.

When using either method, be certain to turn on Frame Blending. Enable it globally in the Composition and on the Time Stretched Layer.

Make It Fit!

Need to make a layer fit? Perhaps you want to scale a vector object Full Screen or you need to make a large photo fit your canvas. After Effects takes the guess work out by giving you three different stretch commands.

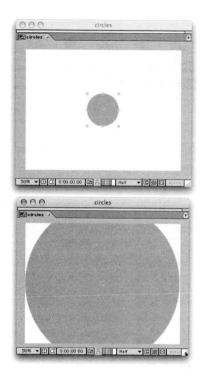

- To stretch a layer to fit: Cmd+Option+F (Ctrl+Alt+F). It's important to note however that option does not preserve the footage's original aspect ratio.

- To stretch a layer to fit horizontally: Cmd+Option+Shift+H (Ctrl+Alt+Shift+H) to preserve the aspect ratio and fit the image horizontally. This will likely leave an empty area above and below the image.

- To stretch a layer to fit vertically: Cmd+Option+Shift+G (Ctrl+Alt+Shift+G) to preserve the aspect ratio and fit the image vertically. This will likely leave an empty area left and right of the image.

Cleaning Up Means Speeding Up

If you've imported multiple projects or your project has slowed down for whatever reason, it's a good idea to do a little housekeeping:

❶ Save your project.

❷ Go to File>Remove Unused Footage to remove all unused footage from the project.

❸ Go to File>Consolidate All Footage to remove duplicate footage items from the project.

❹ If you only want to keep certain compositions within a project, select them from the project window and choose File>Reduce Project. All unselected compositions and files not used in those compositions will be erased.

In a Flash

If you create (or are given) a SWF file to import, After Effects can bring it in like any other footage file via the import box, but there are a few gotchas.

- Be sure you have the latest QuickTime installed as AE uses QuickTime to rasterize the Flash file.

- Make sure the file was published as Flash 5. The newer Flash MX files are not compatible.

- AE sees the footage as Raster, which means you can't scale it up very well. You are best off opening the SWF or FLA file in Flash and sizing it there. Republish to make the Flash move self-contained.

- Profound Effects (http://www.profoundeffects.com/) has an awesome SWF importer that allows you to bring the files in as vectors. Its part of their Useful Things package.

- Remember, most Flash animation is built at 8 or 12 frames per second for faster downloads. It will look choppy when cut into a video frame rate comp.

Streamlining Illustrator Compatibility

Here are quick tips for saving Illustrator files.

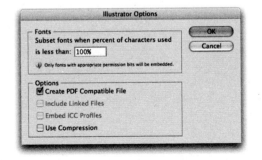

❶ When saving Illustrator files, select the Create PDF Compatible File option in the Illustrator Native Format Options dialog box so that Adobe Illustrator files display correctly in AE.

❷ Save your files in the AI format to make sure layers rasterize properly.

❸ If you plan to work with Zaxwerks Invigorator, you'll need to save an AI v.8 file. Under Illustrator CS choose File>Export and choose Illustrator Legacy from the drop down menu.

Upper or Lower (How To Tell)

If you are using interlaced video (most video is) you may have to decide which field to show first. After Effects will normally do this for you by reading that metadata from the footage upon import. But if things don't look right (or you want to double-check), do the following:

1 Select the footage in the Project window.

2 Choose File>Interpret Footage>Main or press Cmd+F (Ctrl+F).

3 Choose Upper Field First from the Separate Fields pop-up menu. Then click OK.

4 You now must open the item into a footage window. Choose it in the Project window and hold down Option (Alt) while you double-click the footage.

5 Select the Time Controls Window by pressing Cmd+3 (Ctrl+3).

6 Scroll through the Footage window until you find a section with a lot of movement.

7 Click the frame advance button several times. If the motion appears to jump backward every other frame, you have interpreted field wrong. Go back to footage Interpretation and choose Lower Field First.

While many analog capture cards vary, Digital Video (DV) is always lower field first.

Missing the PC/MAC Version of a Font?

If the font you are using is unavailable on the system where you will be animating the text, convert the text to outlines.

1 In Illustrator, select the text by clicking on the layer or press Cmd+A (Ctrl+A) to select all. Go to Type>Create Outlines. Save the file. You may want to choose Save As to preserve an editable version of the file.

2 You won't be able to change the font or text after doing this but the file will open on any system with Illustrator installed. It must be the version the file was created in or later. Outlines can also be pasted as masks between AI and AE if you change your clipboard preference settings to copy as AICB instead of PDF.

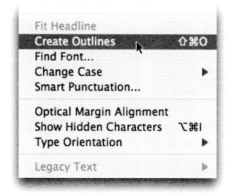

211

Save and Save Again

Do your good saving habits ever come back to haunt you? We are so good at hitting Save that sometimes we save an experiment that we didn't mean to keep. Well with the release of After Effects 6.5, Adobe offers a way to protect yourself from Art Directors, clients, or your own 'bad' ideas.

The new incremental save feature will save the project using the project name and an incremented numeric identifier. For example, IWASCV01.aep would become IWASCV02.aep.

❶   Have a project open and make modifications.

❷   Choose File>Increment and Save.

For Avid Users

No we don't meant rabid fans, we actually mean those folks who are building graphics with sources from Avid editing systems. After Effects 6.5 can actually read and write both OMF and AAF files.

The Open Media Framework (OMF) format is an older format used by earlier Avid systems to facilitate the exchange of files. The Advanced Authoring Format (AAF) is a newer format that is quickly becoming a standard for exchange files for video editing.

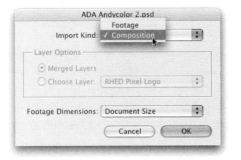

Drag & Drop... Build & Stack

After Effects 6.5 allows Photoshop files to be imported as Comps by simply doing a drag and drop. Instead of assuming you wanted a flattened footage file like earlier versions, AE6.5 gives you a dialog box. Simply choose Composition from the Import Kind drop-down box.

Photoshop & Illustrator Convert

Have you ever imported a PSD file as footage and then had second thoughts? Maybe it would have been to have layers after all. Or part way through an animated logo, the client wants you to break off pieces and animate them individually.

After Effects 6.5 has a new answer just for you:

If you want to do a global replace throughout your project, choose File>Replace Footage>With Layered Comp.

OR

If you want to replace a flattened file with a layered one at a local level, select the layer and choose Layer>Convert to Layered Comp.

Change takes time (at least a little). Give After Effects a few moments to catch up.

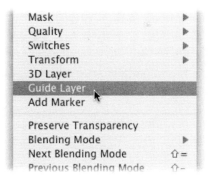

A New Kind of Shy—Guides

After Effects 6.5 gives you better control over designing with templates or guides. It is now possible to have an overlay or template layer enabled in the Timeline and if you flag it properly, AE will skip it for the final render.

Guides are useful to ensure the placement of key design elements. You can use any type of layer as a guide if it helps.

❶ Highlight the intended guide layer in the timeline.

❷ Choose Layer>Guide Layer.

❸ A new icon appears to indicate a guide layer is in use.

❹ In the render settings dialog box, be sure to set guide layers to All Off.

ON THE SPOT

Masks and Mattes:
Using Layers to Hide (and Add)

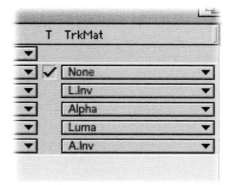

Vastly underused and never to be underestimated, using Masks and Mattes is the key to successful compositing. This chapter presents tips on tried-and-true techniques and also on some of the great new adds like the Auto Trace feature. Hide parts of footage you don't like or use the luminance channel of a layer to affect the alpha channel of another layer.

You can create masks in AE or import them from programs like Photoshop and Illustrator. Masks can be used as motion paths and can be applied to effects with position data. We'll show you how to manage one or multiple masks per layer efficiently and effortlessly (well, almost effortlessly).

Using Mattes means faster compositing. You'll get effects that you just can't achieve any other way.

Masks and Mattes rock!

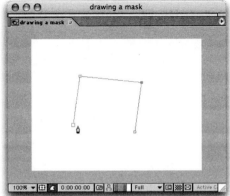

Creating Masks Within AE

To create a mask:

❶ Select any layer, or create a new layer by pressing Cmd+Y (Ctrl+Y).

❷ Click on the Pen Tool in the Tools Palette.

❸ Click anywhere in the composition window to make a vertex point.

❹ Continue clicking to add points.

❺ Return to the first point you made to close the mask. You'll see a circle icon appear next to your Pen Tool to indicate you are closing the mask.

Tools of the Trade

When you click quickly on a layer and make a vertex, you make a corner point vertex. If you click and drag one way or another, the vertex point becomes a smooth point, otherwise known as a Bezier Vertex Point. Bezier vertexes have direction handles that you can tweak while drawing or after you've closed your masks.

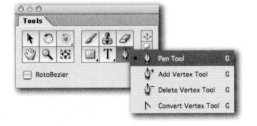

- You can change a vertex from point to smooth (or vise versa) by using the Convert Vertex Tool, which is located beneath the Pen Tool in the Tools Palette.

- You can also press G on the keyboard to toggle between the Pen, Add Vertex, Delete Vertex, or Convert Vertex Tools.

- Hold down the Option+Cmd (Alt+Ctrl) keys to change the Selection Tool into the Convert Vertex Tool.

- Be careful not to have all your points selected because you will convert them all.

- Hold down the Cmd key (Ctrl) over a vertex point to turn the Selection Tool in a Remove Vertex Tool.

- Hold down the Cmd key (Ctrl) anywhere else on the mask to change the Selection Tool to the Add Vertex Tool.

- Option+Click (Alt+Click) to select all points in a mask.

- To invert a mask, press Cmd+Shift+I (Ctrl+Shift+I).

- For a new mask, press Cmd+Shift+N (Ctrl+Shift+N).

RotoBezier Masks

RotoBezier vertexes visually resemble Bezier vertexes because they are curved but RotoBezier vertexes differ in that they don't have handles you can access and manipulate. The RotoBezier option automatically calculates curved segments for you.

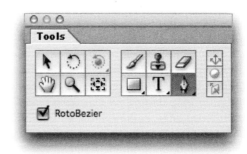

You may find it easier to draw a mask, and then convert it to RotoBezier afterward. There might be a shift in shape if you do so however. You can also change a RotoBezier mask into a Bezier mask, which will not cause any change to the mask shape. RotoBezier vertexes are easier to use while rotoscoping because you don't have to worry about direction handles.

- To draw a RotoBezier mask, click the Pen Tool from the Tools Palette and click RotoBezier. Click and draw in the composition window.

- To convert a mask to a RotoBezier Mask, select the mask in the layer or composition window and choose>Layer>Mask>RotoBezier. You could also select the mask and context click for the flyout menu; choose the RotoBezier option from there.

Open and Closed Masks

Open masks are paths that can be used for several purposes.

They can be used for effects that employ masks like Path Text, Audio Waveform, Audio Spectrum, Stroke, or Vegas.Open masks can be used for effects that have positional attributes like Lens Flare, Spherize, most distort effects.

And open masks can also be used as motion paths.

Most of the time, you'll want to make sure your masks are closed.

- To make sure your mask is closed, select a mask and choose Layer>Mask>Closed.

- You can also select your mask in the composition window and Context click (Right click or Control click) to make sure "closed" has a checkmark by it.

Quick Elliptical or Rectangular Masks

You know you need a mask, and you'd be perfectly happy if it were centered on your layer. Great! Lets save some time.

❶ Select a layer where you'd like to apply a mask.

❷ Double-click on either the Rectangular or Elliptical Mask Tool in the Tools Palette to apply an oval or square mask that fits the layer.

❸ Modify the mask, or use it as is.

Animating Mask Shape

So your mask needs to adjust over time. Don't most things in life? Not a problem. After Effects offers several functions for keyframing your masks. Let's get started by clicking the triangle by the Masks to open up the mask properties.

- Click the Mask Shape stopwatch to set a shape keyframe. You can also press Shift+Option+M (Shift+Alt+M) to set an initial keyframe on a selected mask

- Advance in the Timeline and modify your vertexes to make a new shape keyframe.

- Make the workspace as long as your shape mask animation and RAM preview to see After Effects interpolate the shape transformation.

- When modifying a Bezier handle, you will affect both the incoming and outgoing curves. To access one handle at a time, use the Convert Vertex Tool, and drag one of the handles. You can also hold down the Option key (Alt) to do the same.

- If you want to rejoin your handles, use the Convert Vertex Tool to convert the vertex to linear, then back to Bezier again.

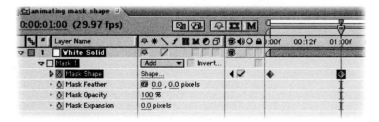

Freely Transform

So you need to tweak the mask? The easiest way we find is with the Free Transform command.

- To scale or rotate a mask, select the mask then choose Layer>Mask>Free Transform Points or press Cmd+T (Ctrl+T). If the mask is not highlighted, these shortcuts will not work.

- Remember that scaling and rotating occur around the anchor point of the mask. Click and drag on the anchor point to move it.

- Placing your curser over one of the corners will turn it into a rotate symbol. Hold the shift key to constrain rotation to 45 percent increments.

- To disable the preview while you rotate or scale, hold down the option key while you transform.

- To scale a side, place your curser over one of the center bounding box points.

- To scale the entire mask, place your curser over one of the corners, slightly further away than where you mouse to invoke rotation. Hold the shift key to constrain the mask's proportion.

- Use Free Transform Points to move a mask, and hold the shift key to constrain movement to the X or Y axis.

- Cmd+Drag (Ctrl+Drag) to scale around anchor point; add the Shift key to keep it proportional.

- Return or ESC (Enter) to Exit Free Transform Mask.

Free Transform Vertices

Free Transform is great for global change, but it can also be applied to selected vertices of a mask, or even selected vertices of more than one mask.

❶   Select any vertices you want to transform. You can shift-click multiple vertices.

❷   Double click to Free Transform Points or press Cmd+T (Ctrl+T).

❸   Press Enter or ESC to apply.

Rotoscoping with Masks

Not handy with a brush? Not crazy about rotoscoping with the Paint Effects? You can do great rotoscoping with masks (although it's tedious.)

- For complex areas, split up the job into a few masks rather than trying to animate one intricate mask.

- If you're going to be adding or deleting vertices you should go to Preferences>General>Persevere Constant Vertex Count When Editing Masks and turn it off. If you delete a point, you will only be affecting that mask shape keyframe, whereas if you leave Preserve Count it on, After Effects will delete that point throughout your layer.

- You should try to maintain your vertex count though. Deleting or adding points to a mask can cause unpredictable interpolation, and can adversely affect motion blur for the mask.

Multiple Mask Organization

Like anything in life, it's possible to have too much of a good thing. If you use multiple masks, a little organization can save you a lot of time.

- Name masks by selecting the mask number, hitting return, type a name and hit return again.

- You can change the default yellow color of masks by clicking on the color square by the mask name and selecting any other color. When you change mask color you can visually identify which masks are doing what over time in the composition window.

- Change the order of the masks by selecting and dragging them up or down in the Timeline or by selecting a mask and hitting Cmd+[(that's a left bracket) or Cmd+] (and that is a right bracket) (Ctrl+[or Ctrl+]) to move down or up a position.

- You can select all the vertices of a mask by selecting the mask name in the layer/source window.

- Delete vertex points by selecting the individual points and clicking the delete key.

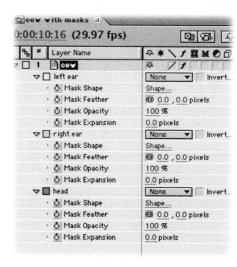

Accessing Mask Properties Quickly

Doesn't feel fast enough? Here are a few power tips to get you working with your masks in a jiffy.

To view all mask properties in the Timeline	MM
Mask Shape in the Timeline	M
Mask Feather in the Timeline	F
Mask Opacity in the Timeline	TT
Mask Shape Dialog Box	Cmd+Shift+M (Ctrl+Shift+M)
Mask Feather Dialog Box	Cmd+Shift+F (Ctrl+Shift+F)

Locking and Hiding Masks

Sometimes you can be your own worst enemy. Using a lot of masks can be troublesome as they can get in your way and be unintentionally modified. If a mask is "locked in," consider locking it down.

1 Twirl down a layer to reveal all of your masks.

2 In the A/V features column, you can lock an individual mask to prevent changes.

To hide those masks, choose Layer>Mask>Hide Locked Masks to hide the vertices in the Comp Window. You will still see the results of the locked masks, but cannot make accidental changes.

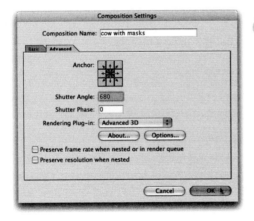

Motion Blur on Masks

Each mask with mask shape keyframes can have motion blur. To apply Motion Blur:

1 Select one or more masks

2 Choose Layer> Masks>Motion Blur and choose one of the Options:

• Same as Layer,—to control the mask's blur using the Motion Blur button.

• On—to render the mask blur even if the Motion Blur button for the layer is not selected.

• Off—to apply no motion blur to the mask.

• Click the Enable Motion Blur button in the Timeline window to view the blur.

The amount of blur is based on the shutter angle of the composition. To change the amount, go to Composition>Composition Settings. In the Advanced Tab, change the Shutter Angle. The input values are 0–720, and higher numbers create more blur.

Showdown: Layer vs. Comp Window

New to AE 6 is the ability to draw and manipulate masks in the composition window. What does the layer window have that the composition window doesn't (and vice versa)?

- In the composition window, you can choose to view masks, or not, by clicking the Toggle View Masks button (which is the third button in, on the bottom left side.)

- It's easier to work on masks in the layer window because you can select your target masks by using the target pop-up menu in the layer window, or in the middle bottom of the window. This way you can choose to edit a mask already on the layer or select Target None to draw a new mask.

You'll find that you'll use both the composition window and layer window while using masks. Use the following shortcuts to get from the layer window to the comp window quickly.

- To switch from the Layer Window to the Comp Window, click the comp window icon in the layer window (lower right button) or click the comp window icon on the Timeline (upper right below comp marker button).

- To switch from the Comp Window to the Layer Window, double click in the Comp Window or select a layer in the timeline and press Return on your Keyboard. You can also double click on any layer in the Timeline to open its Layer Window.

- If your windows are still tabbed, click the Comp Window or Layer Window tabs.

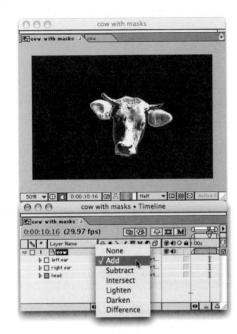

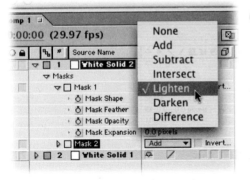

Mask Modes I

Every mask in After Effects has a mode. Select your layer and hit M on your keyboard to show masks. The Mask mode is visible in the switches column.

● The default mask mode is Add, it means the new mask combines with the previous mask on the layer.

● Masks work based on their placement in the timeline so the subtract will subtract the selected area from all masks above it.

● Intersect adds the mask to all masks above it but will only display the area at which all masks intersect.

● Difference adds a mask to all masks above it and displays all masked areas except the areas where masks intersect.

● Use None when using a mask-based effect. A mask set to None will not affect the transparency of a layer.

Mask Modes II

To further enhance a mask, vary the opacity of each mask.

● With Add and Intersect, the opacity of all intersecting masks is added together.

● With Lighten, the mask with the highest opacity is used, so opacity doesn't build up.

● With Darken, where multiple masks intersect, the highest transparency value is used, so transparency doesn't build up.

● Keep in mind, you can't animate mask modes.

Invert Modes

When you mask an area, you are telling After Effects that you want to show the bit you selected while hiding the rest of the layer. You can invert any mask by checking the invert box in the Switches Column. This will hide the area you masked and show the rest of the layer. Like mask modes, you can't animate or change an inverted mask without changing its state for the length of the composition.

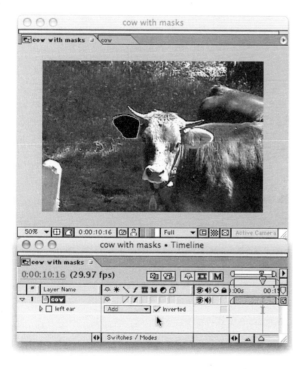

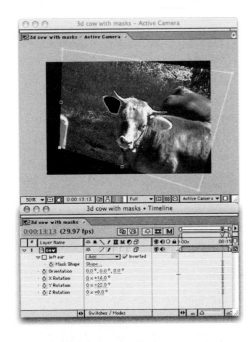

Masks in 3D

Any 3D layer in After Effects can have a mask. Only the layer has 3D properties, however, so you cannot draw a mask on the Z axis. You can draw the mask, then rotate the layer on the Z axis though.

Collapsing Transformations can complicate masks on 3D layers. It's best to leave the collapse switch off.

Using Masks from Illustrator

You can draw a path in Illustrator and paste it directly as a mask in AE. This is handy as you can draw complicated or fun shapes more easily in Illustrator. You can also harness several of Illustrator's built-in shapes, or convert symbols into shapes for use.

❶ In your Illustrator Files Handling & Clipboard preference, make sure you select the AICB option. Go to Illustrator>Preferences>Files Handling & Clipboard>Copy As AICB>Preserve Paths

❷ Create a path in Illustrator, select it, and copy it by choosing Edit>Copy or Cmd+C (Ctrl+C).

❸ Select a layer in After Effects and paste the path into the layer window or composition window by choosing Edit>Paste or Cmd+V (Ctrl+V).

You don't have to save your Illustrator file, but you might want to if you care to access the original path later.

Using Masks from Photoshop

Paths from Photoshop can also be pasted directly into AE as well.

1. In Photoshop, select the Pen Tool and draw either a closed or open path.

2. Switch to the Path Selection Tool to select the whole path.

3. Copy it (choose Edit>Copy) or press Cmd+C (Ctrl+C).

4. Select a layer in After Effects and paste and chose Edit>Paste or press Cmd+V (Ctrl+V).

5. Paste the path into the layer window or composition window.

The Custom Shape Tool in Photoshop is a great way to draw vector shapes. You can copy and paste them into AE like freehand paths.

Animating Type as Masks

It's possible to create type as masks as well.

1. In Illustrator, type a letter in a large point size, then go to Type>Create Outlines.

2. Select the path, copy it, and paste it into AE.

3. Turn on the stopwatch for mask shape.

4. Go back into Illustrator and type a different letter and do the same, but this time, in AE move about a few frames down in the Timeline before pasting your type.

5. Make sure you have Mask Shape selected in the Timeline. AE automatically makes another mask shape keyframe.

6. Do a RAM Preview, and see AE morph from one letter to another!

Watch out for letters with negative areas as they will paste as more than one mask. Try animating the opacity of the new masks to sync with your morph. You also may want to give Smart Mask Interpolation a try.

Masks as Motion Paths

Need to animate complicated motion paths or have an object move around your client's logo? You can paste Illustrator and Photoshop masks as motion paths in much the same way you can paste them as masks.

1 In Illustrator or Photoshop, draw a path and copy it.

2 In After Effects select a layer and hit P to bring up the Position Transform property.

3 Paste the path.

Paths can also be pasted into other spatial properties like Anchor Point or any effect that has keyframeable spatial properties. Make sure to select the property either in the layer name or source name column. Try this with a simple arc path and paste the path into the Lens Flare>Flare Center property.

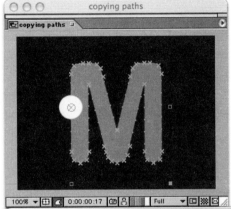

The keyframes in the motion path will automatically be set to rove in time to create a constant velocity along the path. You can adjust the default duration of two seconds by dragging the first or last keyframe to a new point in time.

Besides Illustrator paths, you can also paste paths from Photoshop and After Effects itself

Smart Mask Interpolation (Pro)

If you're animating Mask Shape and not getting quite the results you want, it's time for a new tool. Select your mask shape keyframes and go to Window>Smart Mask Interpolation.

Mask shapes tend not to animate smoothly. Smart Mask Interpolation creates intermediate keyframes based on the settings you choose to create smoother mask shape transformations. You can modify settings in the submenu (click on the arrow on the top right of the palette).

By default After Effects matches the first vertex. A good thing to do if you're still not getting a smooth animation is to line-up the first vertex of a path. (Thanks to Trish and Chris Meyers for this tip). Choose your first mask shape keyframe, and notice that one of the vertices is slightly bigger than the others. This is the first vertex. Move to the second keyframe and notice it's the first vertex.

Choose a vertex that more closely resembles the first mask shape's first vertex and choose Layer>Mask>Set First Vertex to designate a new first vertex.

The simplified default settings in Smart Mask Interpolation are decent, and should improve interpolation. Modifying the settings yourself can help but ultimately the best thing is to use two mask shapes that are somewhat similar.

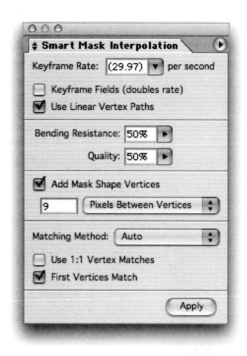

The Pen Tool and Motion Paths

Once you have a motion path, you can use the Pen tool to add keyframes.

❶   Select a layer with a motion path.

❷   Choose the Pen Tool from the Tools Palette.

❸   Click on the path to add keyframes.

❹   Chose the Selection Tool from the Tools Palette or hold down the Cmd Key (Ctrl) to change the Pen Tool to the Selection Tool, and move these new keyframes to new positions.

When you add keyframes to a motion path by using the Pen Tool you may want to rove the resulting keyframes in time to maintain constant velocity.

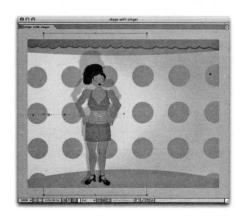

Trouble Pasting?

Pasting Masks as paths has become much more complex in AE6. After drawing your path (in Photoshop, Illustrator, or AE) and copying it to the clipboard, paste it onto the appropriate layer. It will sometimes paste as a Mask, not a path (even if you select the word Position before pasting it). The solution:

❶ With the layer selected, type M and select the Mask Shape property.

❷ Cut to the clipboard by pressing Cmd+x (Ctrl+x).

❸ Select the Position property and paste by pressing Cmd+V (Ctrl+V)Cmd+v (Ctrl+v).

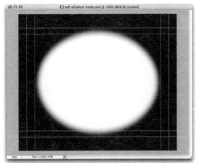

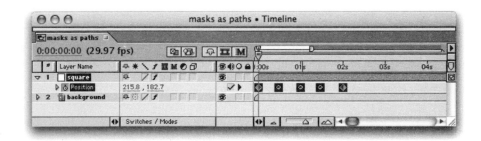

Make Your Own Mattes

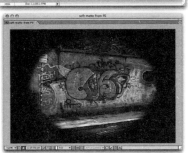

Mattes can be still or motion layers. Create your own mattes in Photoshop. Go to File>New>and choose a resolution of the layer you want to affect.

In both alpha channel mattes and luminance mattes, darker (black) pixels will be transparent and lighter (white) pixels will be opaque. Intermediate shades will produce partial transparency. For soft edges on a matte, use a diffuse brush, run the Gaussian Blur filter, or feather your edges.

Mask Effects

We hope you like using masks because certain effects rely heavily on them.

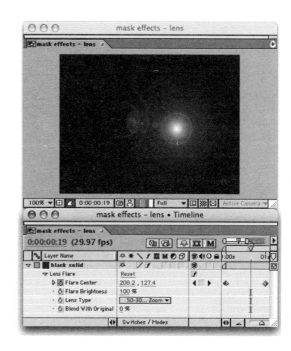

Standard Version:

- Path Text
- Audio Waveform
- Audio Spectrum
- Stroke Fill (closed paths only)
- Smear (closed paths only)

Pro Version:

- Reshape (closed paths only)
- Vegas
- Inner Outer Key (closed paths only)
- Particle Playground can also use a mask shape to define effect boundaries

Certain effects have positional attributes into which path data can be pasted

- Lens Flare
- Spherize
- Most distort effects

Panning in a Mask

Need to keep your masks stable but pan your layer? Select a masked layer and choose the Pan Behind Tool from the Tools Palette or press Y. Make sure you are in the composition window and click inside the masked area to move the displayed information.

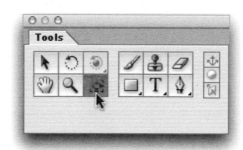

Notice the masks have moved in the layer window, but not in the comp window. You have actually completed two steps in one by changing the position of your layer and the shape of your masks.

Contain Yourself (Track Mattes)

Ever found yourself needing boundaries? We don't mean rules or a schedule to follow, but rather graphical walls to contain an element. Perhaps you want to take footage of an ocean and have it show through letters, or you want the shape of a client's logo to contain a data stream. That's what track mattes are for.

❶ Be sure that you see modes in your timeline (if not click the Switches/Modes button at the bottom of the window).

❷ Position the two layers in your timeline so the matte layer (the one that cuts) is directly above the fill layer. Be sure there are no gaps between the fill and matte layers.

❸ In the TrkMat drop down menu, pick one of the following methods to define transparency.

- Alpha Matte. Areas with 100 percent alpha channel are opaque.

- Alpha Inverted Matte. Areas with 0 percent alpha channel are opaque.

- Luma Matte. Areas with 100 percent luminance pixels are opaque.

- Luma Inverted Matte. Areas with 100 percent luminance pixels are opaque.

When the track matte feature is turned on, the matte layer's visibility is disabled. You can turn it back on, but that usually defeats the purpose. You still have the ability to manipulate and resize the layer, and its transformations will carry through to the matte.

A Better Track Matte

Do you need to use a layer's alpha channel to cut a hole in the layer below? Easy, right? Use a track matte. But that only works on the layer immediately below. If you have multiple layers to affect, choose to use Stencil or Silhouette mode.

❶   Active the Modes panel in the Timeline window.

❷   Click on the mode list and choose one of the following.

•   Choose Stencil Alpha to create a stencil using the top layer's alpha channel. This will make all areas of the lower layers transparent except where the object above used to be opaque

•   Choose Silhouette Alpha to create a silhouette using the layer's alpha channel. This will cut a transparent hole where the top layer was opaque.

Don't have an alpha channel? You can also create Stencils and Silhouettes based on the top layer's luma values.

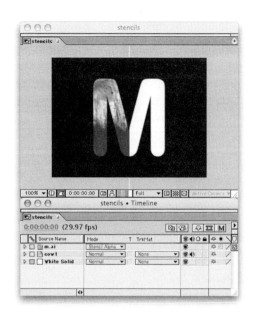

Handling Track Mattes

Mattes are great, but learn to control them.

•   If the track matte layer is taking up precious room in the Timeline, you may want to hide this layer. Press the Shy button for the layer, and turn on the Shy button for the composition.

•   If you animate the position, rotation, or anchor point of the affected layer, parent your layers so the track matte layer follows its mate.

•   Apply a levels filter to the track matte layer to boost contrast or to animate the opacity of the matte.

•   You can also use nested compositions as track mattes!

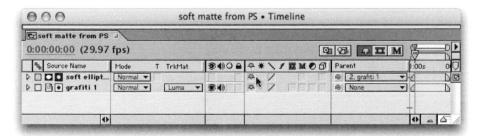

ON THE SPOT

Express Yourself:

Harnessing the Power of Expressions

If you're a designer or animator, and you've thought about tiptoeing into the world of programming, we'd like to introduce you to Javascript. Javascript has become the unofficial language of graphics applications, including Photoshop, Illustrator, Flash, Web browsers, and (of course) After Effects.

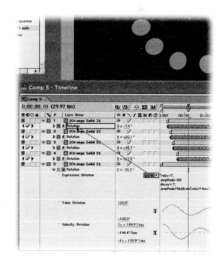

The good news is that you don't have to master Javascript to write AE Expressions. You just need to learn a little bit, and then you can learn more if you'd like to delve really deeply into the language. But with just a few Javascript phrases, you can boost your animations to a new level.

Expressions are mostly used when keyframing would be difficult, like when you want to add a huge amount of random motion to a layer. They can also link properties together, so that one property controls another.

If you're intrigued, read on...

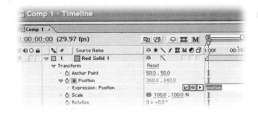

Express Yourself

Expressions are small Javascript programs that can control layer properties (an alternative to keyframing). To create simple expressions, you don't need to know how to program Javascript.

To add an expression to any property, reveal it in the Timeline, then Option click (Alt click) the property's stopwatch. Add expressions to effect properties by Option clicking (Alt clicking) their stopwatches in the Effect Control palette. To delete expressions, Option click (Alt click) stopwatches a second time. To temporarily disable an expression, click the equal-sign button that appears to the left of the stopwatch for any property that's controlled by an expression.

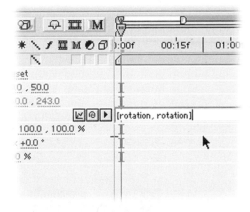

Finishing an Expression

When you finish creating an expression (either by using the Pickwhip tool or by hand typing), click the mouse in a blank (gray) area of the Timeline or press the Enter key on the numeric keypad. Don't press the Return (Enter) key on the main keyboard because After Effects will think you want to add another line to the expression.

Time Expressions

Create a small solid and animate it moving around in the comp. Duplicate the layer and remove the keyframes (by clicking the Position stopwatch) from the top copy. Also on the top copy, add the following expression to the Position property:

thisComp.layer(thisLayer,+1).position.valueAtTime(time-.5)

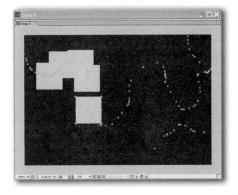

Duplicate the top copy three times, play the comp and you'll see four layers following the original layer, like a trail. This works because each layer is referring to the position property of the layer below it–layer(thisLayer,+1).position. But after the word position, the phrase valueAtTime(time–.5) means set this layer's position to the position of where the layer below it was half a second ago. Try playing with the .5 to change how close the layers follow each other. If you change it to 2, the layers will be further apart. If you change it to .1, they'll be very close together.

Soloing Expressions

To solo all expressions on the selected layer (or layers), type EE (type the E key twice, rapidly). Type EE again to hide the expressions. If an expression is more than one line long, you may have to adjust the Timeline to see it all. Position your mouse-pointer on the line directly under the expression. When you see a double-headed arrow, drag downward to see more of the expression.

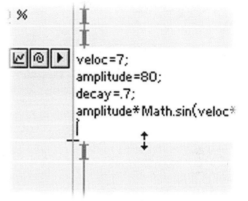

Control and Controller

Many expressions link two properties together in a relationship similar to parenting, in which one property controls another property. For instance, if you added an expression to a mask's Expansion property, then Pickwhipped the layer's Opacity property, Opacity would control Expansion.

You can always add the expression to the controlled property (in this case Expansion), and then Pickwhip (or indicate by typing) the controller. Then, to cause change over time, animate the controller (in this case Opacity). If you link Expansion and Opacity in this way, then animate Opacity so the layer fades in over time, the mask will expand automatically as the layer is fading.

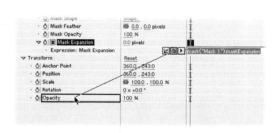

Pickwhipping I

To make a layer's position control its scale (so that it changes size as it moves), add an expression to its scale property, then select its position property by dragging the Pickwhip from position to the word scale.

When you animate changes in position, scale will change too. You can also Pickwhip a property on another layer. For instance, to make layer A's opacity control layer B's rotation, add an expression to layer B's rotation property, then drag the Pickwhip to layer A's opacity property. When you animate changes to layer A's opacity, layer B's rotation will change too.

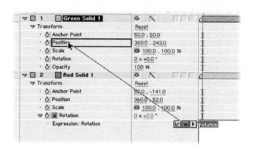

You can also Pickwhip effect properties. For instance, try adding the Basic Text and Fast Blur effects to a layer. Animate changes to Basic Text's Tracking property. Add an expression to Fast Blur's Blurriness property and Pickwhip Basic Text's Tracking property. As the text tracks out, it gets blurrier. As it tracks back in, it gets sharper.

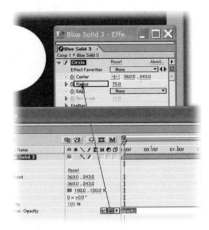

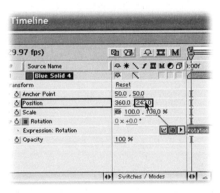

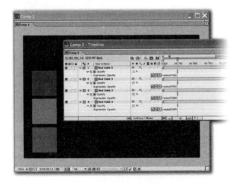

Pickwhipping II

To Pickwhip an effect property, you don't need to reveal that property in the Timeline. Instead, just drag the Pickwhip to the Effect Controls window, and click a property there.

Pickwhipping III

Some properties, such as position, are two-dimensional, meaning they are controlled by two values. Position is controlled by an X value and a Y value. (If you're working in 3D, position is three-dimensional, controlled by X, Y, and Z). Scale is also two dimensional, controlled by width and height. On the other hand, Opacity and Rotation are one-dimensional, each being controlled by a single value. In the case of Opacity, this is a percent, whereas for Rotation, it's an angle (degrees).

What happens when you create an expression in which a two-dimensional property controls a one-dimensional property? For instance, what if you try to control Rotation with Position? Position will send two numbers to Rotation, but Rotation will only use one of those numbers and throw the other one away. By default, Rotation will use the X and ignore the Y.

If you want Rotation to change when the Y changes (when the layer moves up or down), add an expression to Rotation, then Pickwhip just the Y dimension of Position.

Randomizing

Wiggle chooses random values on certain frames (designated by the how often number), but in between those frames, it smoothly interpolates (just as if the random values were keyframes). Sometimes, you want After Effects to choose a new random value on each frame. For example, you might want to randomize opacity to create a flicker. Or, you might want to randomize the Direction property of the Directional Blur effect, so that on each frame, the blurriness runs in a different direction. Here's an expression you can add to any property which will randomize it frame-by-frame:

random(100);

On each frame, this expression will choose a different number, between zero and whatever number is inside the parentheses (in this case 100).

Another Dimension

When you add an expression to a one-dimensional property, such as Opacity and Pickwhip a two-dimensional property, such as Scale, After Effects will add a bracketed number to the end of the expression: scale[0]. The zero refers to scale's first dimension, which is width. If you replace the zero with a one (scale[1]), Opacity will be controlled by height instead of width.

Along these lines, position[0] means X, position[1] means Y, and if you're working in 3D, position[2] means Z. And, the same holds true for any positionable effect property, such as the Flare Center of a Lens Flare Effect.

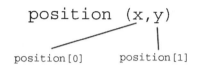

Expression Arithmetic I

You can add simple arithmetic to the end of expressions to make them stronger, weaker or to flip them to their opposites. For instance, if you add an expression to Rotation and Pickwhip Opacity, you can then click to the right of the last character of the expression and type +50. The expression will then read Opacity+50. Without the arithmetic, if the Opacity was 100 percent, Rotation would be 100 degrees. With the arithmetic, Rotation will be 150 degrees.

Similarly, you can subtract from an expression by tacking –50 (or some other number) to its end. You can also multiply and divide by typing *50 or /50 at the end of the expression. There are no multiplication and division symbols on computer keyboards, so you have to use an asterisk for multiplication and a forward-slash for division.

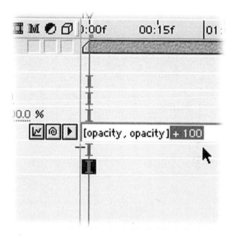

Expression Arithmetic II

Multiply any number by negative one, and you get its opposite. For instance 100 times negative one is -100. On the other hand, -25 times negative one is 25 (positive 25). You can use this math trick to flip expressions to their opposites.

If you add an expression to Rotation and Pickwhip Position, the layer will rotate clockwise when you animate it moving to the right. What if you want it to move counterclockwise? Just multiply the expression by negative one. It will then read "position[0]*–1", and the layer will rotate counterclockwise when you animate its position to the right.

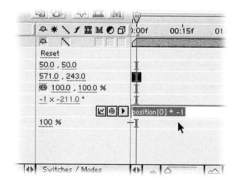

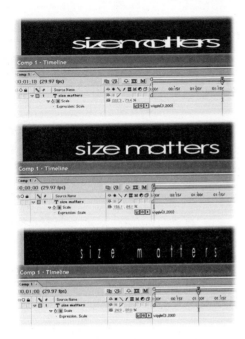

The Incredibly Useful Wiggle

The wiggle expression works much like The Wiggler assistant. While The Wiggler inserts random keyframes into the timeline to grunge up a boring animation, wiggle, being an expression, controls randomness through a text command. This makes it easier to update than The Wiggler. Simply change the expression, and the amount (or frequency) of randomness will change.

For instance, to add wiggle to Scale, Option click (Alt Click) Scale's stopwatch, delete the default expression and type the following:

wiggle(3,25)

The three inside the parentheses sets frequency—or how many times per second you want to randomize Scale. The 25 sets the amount of wiggle, so in this example the Scale will change by 25 percent (bigger or smaller) each time it wiggles (three times per second). If you want Scale to wiggle more often, change the first number, i.e., wiggle(10,25). If you want Scale to change size by a larger amount when it wiggles, change the second number, i.e., wiggle(3,100).

The general formula for this effect is wiggle(how often,how much). Just change how often and how much to whatever numbers you want to try, and see what the expression does. If you don't like the result, plug in different numbers.

Have fun wiggling everything. It can add life to your animations. Wiggle Position, Opacity, Text Size or Tracking, Color properties or Blurriness.

Mapping Value Ranges

Say you want a layer to rotate one time around as it travels from left to right, all the way across the comp. In this case, rotation values will run from zero to 360 degrees.

Assuming this is a 4:3 NTSC comp, X position values will run from zero to 720. If you simply add an expression to Rotation and Pickwhip position, you won't get what you want, because when the layer is at 720, it will also be rotated to 720 degrees, which is double the amount you intended.

The following expression will take the Position range—zero to 720—and map it to the Rotation range—zero to 360—so when the layer is positioned at 720, its rotation will only be 360.

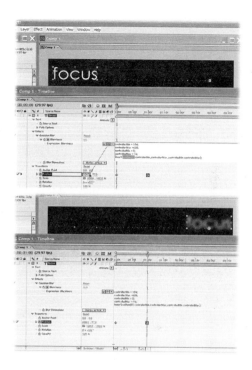

controllerMin = 0;

controllerMax =720;

controlledMin = 0;

controlledMax = 360;

linear(position[0],controllerMin,controllerMax,controlledMin,controlledMax);

To add this expression, Option click (Alt click) the Rotation stopwatch, delete the default expression (rotation), and hand type the new one, pressing Return (Enter) after each line. Click Enter on the numeric keypad when you're finished.

If you change the position animation so that the layer ends at 500x (but still want the layer to rotate one time around), change the second line of the expression to controllerMax = 500;

Naming Names

Many expressions refer to layer names. In other words, the layer names are part of the text of the expressions. If you change layer names after adding an expression, the expression will not automatically update and use the new name. If an expression references an old name, it won't work any more. So it's best to name your layers before adding expressions to them.

Colorful Expressions I

To wiggle color (randomly to any possible color), use the following expression, applied to a Color property of an effect. For example, you can apply this expression to the Color property of the Fill effect (Render>Fill), which fills all the visible pixels of a layer with a solid color:

seedRandom(1,true);

howOften = 2;

r=wiggle(howOften,1)[0];

g=wiggle(howOften,1)[1];

b=wiggle(howOften,1)[2];

a=1;

[r,g,b,a]

To change how often the wiggles occur, change the 2 in the second line of the expression to a higher or lower number to specify how many wiggles per second you'd like.

To wiggle Alpha as well as color, change the line that reads a=1 to

a=wiggle(howOften,1)[3];

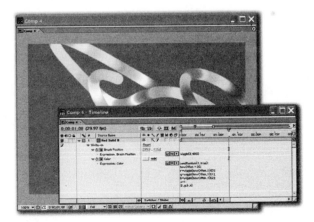

Colorful Expressions II

Expressions think of color as percentage values for the red, green, blue and alpha channels, and the percentages are always numbers between (and including) zero and one. If green is set to .5, that's the same as 50 percent green (or 128 green if you're using the zero to 255 range for RGB values). If you want an expression that wiggles random colors –but you only want random greens hues–try the following:

```
seedRandom(1,true);

howOften = 2;

r=0;

g=wiggle(howOften,1)[1];

b=0;

a=1;

[r,g,b,a]
```

If you want to choose only shades of gray, try this:

```
seedRandom(1,true);

howOften = 2;

r= wiggle(howOften,1)[0];

g=wiggle(howOften,1)[0];

b=wiggle(howOften,1)[0];

a=1;

[r,g,b,a]
```

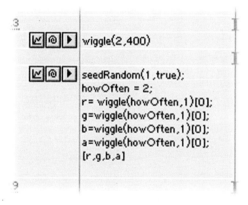

You can use this expression to generate interesting random gradients, if you apply the 4-color Gradient effect (in the Render category) to a solid. Add the expression to each of the four Color properties, changing the seedRandom value to a different number each time. For more fun, add a wiggle expression to the color positions (the Point 1 through Point 4 properties).

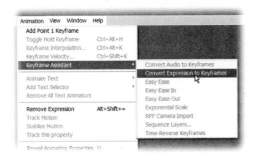

Converting Expressions to Keyframes

Expressions are great, but sometimes keyframes are better, such as when you want to manually adjust easing. Well, you can have your cake and eat it too! You can type or Pickwhip an expression, then convert it to keyframes. Just click the property name (the property to which you added the expression) in the Timeline and choose

Animation>Keyframe Assistants>Convert Expression to Keyframes. The good news is that After Effects will generate keyframes for your expression values. Even better news is that After Effects will not delete your expression. It will just disable your expression. To re-enable the expression, click the not-equal sign button next to the stopwatch. To delete keyframes, click the stopwatch.

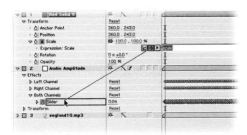

Audio Levels to Keyframes

You can use audio levels (volume) to control other properties, via expressions, but first you must convert audio levels to keyframes, or rather let After Effects do it for you.

Select the audio layer and choose Animation>Keyframe Assistants>Convert Audio to Keyframes. After Effects will add a Null layer (named Audio Amplitude) to comp. Select this layer and press U on your keyboard. The layer will twirl open, revealing three effect properties (assuming you're using stereo sound): Left Channel Slider, Right Channel Slider, and Both Channels Slider. You can use these properties as controllers for expressions.

If you add a small Solid to your comp and add an expression to its Scale property, you can then Pickwhip the Both Channels Slider property of the Null layer. As the music gets louder, the Solid will grow; as the music gets quieter, the Solid will shrink.

If the Solid doesn't grow big enough to suit your tastes (maybe because the audio never gets very loud) try adding a * 2 to the end of the expression. This means "times two," and it multiplies the expression by two, doubling the scale changes. If the solid still doesn't grow enough, change the 2 to a larger number.

Expression Controls I

If you have 30 layers and a wiggle expression on the Position property of each one, it's a pain to adjust wiggle. If the expressions all read wiggle(3,10) and you want to change them all to wiggle(3,1000), you'll have to edit each one separately, one by-one. You can speed things up by using Expression Controls, which are on the Effects menu. You may have tried applying them before and scratched your head when they didn't appear to do anything. By themselves, they don't do anything, but used in conjunction with expressions, they're really powerful and fun. Try this:

❶ Create two layers, a small Solid and a Null. Name the Null "Controller."

❷ With Controller selected, choose Effect>Expression Controls>Slider Control from the menu.

❸ In the Effect Controls panel, select the Slider Control effect and press Return (Enter). Then type to rename the effect "How Often".

❹ Repeat steps 2 and 3, adding another Slider Control, naming this one "How Much."

❺ Select the Solid layer and add an expression to its Position property.

❻ Delete the default expression and type the following (don't end the expression when you're done typing): wiggle(

❼ Drag the Pickwhip tool to the Effect Controls palette and click the "How Often" slider (click the word Slider under the effect name). The expression should now read wiggle(thisComp.layer("Null 1").effect("How Often")("Slider")

❽ Type a comma at the end of the expression, after the final close parenthesis.

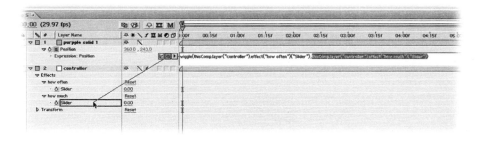

Pickwhip the "How Much" Slider in the Effect Controls window.

Type a closing parenthesis at the very end of the expression (it should end with two closed parentheses).

Finish the expression by pressing Enter on the numeric keypad. The whole expression should read as follows:

wiggle(thisComp.layer("Null 1").effect("How Often")("Slider"),thisComp.layer("Null 1").effect("How Much")("Slider"))

Duplicate the Solid layer (not the Null) many times.

Drag each duplicate to a different location in the Comp window, so they are scattered about the screen.

If you play the comp now, the Solids won't move, because their Positions are controlled by wiggle expressions which are, in turn, controlled by the sliders on the Controller layer. Those sliders are both set, by default, to zero, so nothing is happening.

Adjust both sliders to values greater than zero, play the comp and watch the fun. Keep messing with the sliders and replaying the comp to see the result. Try turning on the stopwatch for one or both sliders and animating their values from zero to a bigger number.

Expression Controls II

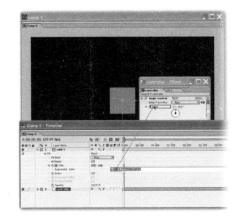

Expression controls are really useful when working with color. Say you have many text layers in your composition and you're working with a client who keeps changing his mind about text color. (Sound familiar?). Every time he says, "Can you make the text white?" you have to change each text layer's color to white, one-by-one.

Then, when he says, "I changed my mind; make them green," you have to change them all again. To save pulling out your hair or his, try adding a Null layer and naming it Controller. Add the Angle Control effect (in the Expression Controls category) to Controller. Rename the effect Color Picker. Finally, add an expression to each Text Color property, always Pickwhipping the Color Picker Angle Control on in the Effect Controls palette. Now, when you adjust the Color Picker Angle Control, all the text colors will change at once to a new color.

Where to Find Expressions

Expressions can get quite complex and mathematical. If you're not a mathematician, you'll be happy to know you can rely on other people for useful expressions. Since they are just text commands, it's easy to copy other people's expressions, and paste them into your comps. Great sources of expressions can be found at the following sites:

www.jjgifford.com/expressions

home.comcast.net/~debberts/web-pages/welcome.html

www.adobeforums.com/cgi-bin/webx?14@29.zclHbRRLO5H.1@.ef91115

www.adobeforums.com/cgi-bin/webx?14@29.zclHbRRLO5H.0@.ef366e7

Useful expressions are frequently posted by Dan Ebberts (and others) on the creativecow After Effects forum.

http://www.creativecow.net/index.php?forumid=2

See Dan Ebbert's expression tutorials here:

http://www.creativecow.net/articles/aftereffects.html#danebberts

In addition to these web resources, Total Training's excellent DVD training series at www.totaltraining.com ships with an e-book of useful expressions.

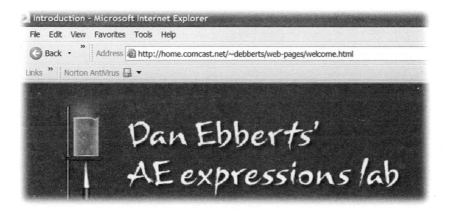

Useful Expressions I

From Total Training:

Circle Fun by and Michael Natkin and Brian Maffitt

This generates perfectly circular motion centered around the original position of a layer. I recommend that you map the radius and cycle inputs to Expression Control sliders, and the phase input to an Expression Control angle.

Apply this expression to the position of the layer.

radius = 75; // the radius of the circle

cycle = 1; // number of seconds to complete a circle; higher value = slower

if (cycle == 0) {cycle = 0.001;} //avoids a "divide by zero" error

phase = 27; // initial angle in degrees from bottom

reverse = 1; // 1 for ccw, -1 for cw

X = Math.sin(reverse * degrees_to_radians(time * 360 / cycle + phase));

Y = Math.cos(degrees_to_radians(time * 360 / cycle + phase));

add(mul(radius, [X,Y]),position)

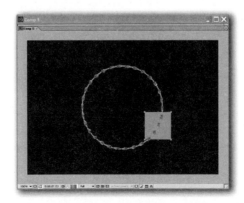

Useful Expressions II

Pendulum By Dan Ebberts

This is an expression you can use to generate a decaying pendulum motion.

The pendulum consists of a rectangular solid and a square solid with a circular mask applied. The anchor point of the rectangular solid has been moved to the upper edge. The square solid is parented to the retangular solid.

Apply the following expression to the rotation property of the rectangular solid:

freq = 1.0; //oscillations per second

amplitude = 50;

decay = 0.7;

amplitude*Math.sin(freq*time*2*Math.PI)/Math.exp(decay*time)

Adjust the velocity, amplitude and decay parameters to suit your needs

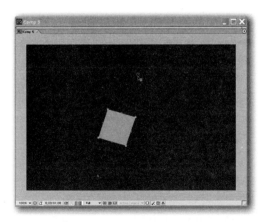

Useful Expressions III

Random Motion by Dan Ebberts

These are the basic expressions for generating random motion. These expressions independently generate random values for position, scale, rotation, and opacity and move to the new values at a random speed.

The expressions can easily be adapted for other properties and effects, 1D or 3D motion, etc.

This is the expression for position:

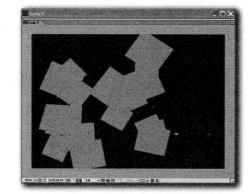

```
segMin = .3; //minimum segment duration
segMax = .7; //maximum segment duration
minVal = [0.1*thisComp.width, 0.1*thisComp.height];
maxVal = [0.9*thisComp.width, 0.9*thisComp.height];

end = 0;
j = 0;
while ( time >= end){
  j ++;
  seedRandom(j,true);
  start = end;
  end += random(segMin,segMax);
}
endVal =  random(minVal,maxVal);
seedRandom(j-1,true);
dummy = random(); //this is a throw-away value
startVal =  random(minVal,maxVal);
ease(time,start,end,startVal,endVal)
```

Adjust segMin and segMax to set the range of times it will take to move from one position to the next.

This is the expression for rotation:

```
segMin = .3; //minimum segment duration
segMax = .7; //maximum segment duration
minVal = -720;
maxVal = 720;

end = 0;
j = 0;
while ( time >= end){
  j ++;
  seedRandom(j,true);
  start = end;
  end += random(segMin,segMax);
}
endVal =  random(minVal,maxVal);
seedRandom(j-1,true);
dummy = random(); //this is a throw-away value
startVal =  random(minVal,maxVal);
ease(time,start,end,startVal,endVal)
```

This is the expression for scale:

```
segMin = .3; //minimum segment duration
segMax = .7; //maximum segment duration
minVal = 50;
maxVal = 200;

end = 0;
j = 0;
while ( time >= end){
  j ++;
  seedRandom(j,true);
  start = end;
  end += random(segMin,segMax);
```

```
}
s = random(minVal,maxVal);
endVal = [s,s];
seedRandom(j-1,true);
dummy = random(); //this is a throw-away value
s = random(minVal,maxVal);
startVal = [s,s];
ease(time,start,end,startVal,endVal)
```

This is the expression for opacity:

```
segMin = .3; //minimum segment duration
segMax = .7; //maximum segment duration
minVal = 10;
maxVal = 100;

end = 0;
j = 0;
while ( time >= end){
  j ++;
  seedRandom(j,true);
  start = end;
  end += random(segMin,segMax);
}
endVal =  random(minVal,maxVal);
seedRandom(j-1,true);
dummy = random(); //this is a throw-away value
startVal =  random(minVal,maxVal);
ease(time,start,end,startVal,endVal)
```

Useful Expressions IV

Color Wheel by Marcus Geduld

This expression creates a color wheel with harmonious (matching) colors.

Create a small square solid (maybe 50pix by 50pix) of any color and move it near the top of the comp. Move its Anchor Point so that it's in the center of the comp (as if the solid was the number twelve on a clock and its Anchor Point was the center of the clock). Apply the Fill effect (render category) to the solid. Rename the solid "Base Color."

Duplicate the Solid. (The dup should be directly above the original in the Timeline layer stack. Don't move it in the comp window!) and rename the dup "Color Stop."

Add the following expression to the dup's Rotation property:

degreeStop = 30;

thisComp.layer(thisLayer,+1).rotation + degreeStop;

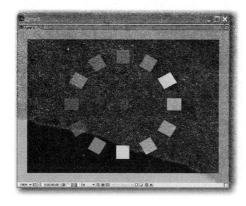

Add the following expression to the dup's Color property (a property of the Fill Effect, which should also be applied to the dup, since you applied it to the original before you duplicated it):

hueOffsetDegree = 30;

layerBelowColor=thisComp.layer(thisLayer,+1).effect("Fill")("Color");

layerBelowHsl = rgbToHsl(layerBelowColor);

layerBelowHue = layerBelowHsl[0];

layerBelowHueDegree = layerBelowHue * 360;

thisLayerHueDegree = layerBelowHueDegree + hueOffsetDegree;

thisLayerHue = thisLayerHueDegree / 360;

thisLayerHsl = [thisLayerHue,1,.5,1]

hslToRgb(thisLayerHsl);

Finally, duplicate this layer (the dup) ten times, which should give you a total of twelve layers.

Try adjusting the Fill Color of the original layer ("Base Color"). The colors of all the other layers should change automatically.

> More bonus tips and updates are available online at www.cmpbooks.com. To receive e-mail updates you can also send a blank e-mail to ae6ots@news.cmpbooks.com.

ON THE SPOT

AE and DVD:
Creating Still and Motion Menus with After Effects

It's amazing what we can do with personal computers these days. Not only can we create original material, but also we now have complete control from concept to distribution.

Back in 1999 (cue sepia-toned memories), once we had edited a video or created an animation we had to output to tape. Now we can output beautiful digital quality without having to worry about generation loss.

Do you know that you can design menus and overlays right in After Effects? Whether you're creating DVD's for training purposes or distributing your latest film, this chapter will teach you to work efficiently with AE and your DVD authoring application.

Overlays from AE

If you designed a menu in AE, and also need a highlight layer, here's what to do.

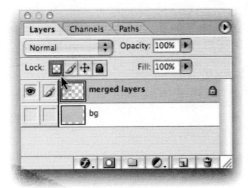

1 Go to an appropriate frame and choose Composition>Save Frame As>Photoshop Layers.

2 Open the file in Photoshop.

3 Turn off the visibility icon for all layers which are not part of the Overlay

4 Select one of the visible layers, and choose Merge Visible from the layer palette submenu.

5 Lock the transparency for this new merged layer by clicking on the Lock transparent pixels box.

6 Choose Edit>Fill and fill with Black (or White, depending on your DVD application).

7 Create a new Empty layer and place it in the background.

8 Select All and Fill this layer with White (or Black, again depending on your DVD application.

9 Delete any unused layers.

10 Choose File>Save As and save a flattened PICT or TARGA file to create an overlay layer. Again, you don't need to save layers or alpha channels.

11 Save the layered PSD file in case you have changes.

Things To Consider

Good menus start with good design decisions.

- When designing your DVD menus, or doing any sort of titling, lean toward a sans serif font, such as Arial or Impact, which are easier to read.

- If the background will be moving, or has a pattern, put a drop shadow or glow on your text for a contrasting edge. Although you don't have to worry about being broadcast safe, stay away from saturated colors like bright reds and yellows.

- Don't forget about safe areas–10 percent for Action Safe and 20 percent for title safe.

Designing in Photoshop CS

To start designing a DVD menu, open Photoshop CS:

❶ Go to File>New.

❷ Click on the presets button, and choose NTSC DV 720x480 (with guides). There is no longer a DVD template in Photoshop, but this is the right size.

❸ Under the advanced tab, choose not to color-manage the file and make sure the pixel aspect ratio is D1/DV NTSC (0.9).

❹ Click OK.

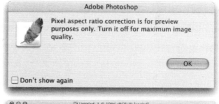

You will be prompted, "Pixel Aspect ratio correction is for preview purposes only. Turn it off for maximum image quality."

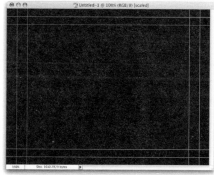

It's fantastic to be able to design in 720x480 as compared to originating in 720x534 and then resizing. The downside is that your image will look slightly aliased. To turn pixel aspect ratio correction off: Go to View>Pixel Aspect Ratio Correction and turn it off. Things will look distorted on the computer (but fine on TV). Your text will be easier to read, which is a plus. Future Photoshop versions will hopefully improve the Pixel Aspect Ratio preview.

468 x 60 web banner

720 x 540 Std. NTSC 601
✓ 720 x 534 Std. NTSC DV/DVD
864 x 486 Wide NTSC 601
864 x 480 Wide NTSC DV/DVD
768 x 576 Std. PAL
1024 x 576 Wide PAL
1280 x 720 HDTV 720P
1920 x 1080 HDTV 1080i

A4

Designing in Photoshop 7 (Step 1)

Unlike Photoshop CS, Photoshop 7 does not offer pixel aspect ratio correction, which makes designing a two-part process.

To start designing a DVD menu in Photoshop 7:

- Go to Photoshop>Color Settings and turn color management off.
- Go to File>New.
- Click on the presets button, and choose 720x534 Std. NTSC DV/DVD.
- Make sure your mode is RGB Color.
- Click OK.

Make your own title safe guides:

1. Go to View>Rulers.
2. Select>All or press Cmd+A (Ctrl+A).
3. Select>Transform Selection.
4. In the option bar for the selection, link the width and height together and scale the selection to 90 percent.
5. Drag four guides to each edge of the selection for action safe.
6. Without hitting return, change the value of the scale of the selection to 80 percent.
7. Drag out four more guides to each edge of the selection for title safe.
8. Press ESC to drop the transformation and go to Select>Deselect to clear the selection.

Design your menu.

Designing in Photoshop 7 (Step 2)

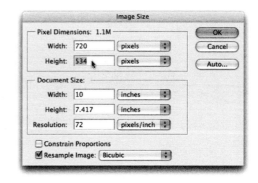

Once your design is complete, you'll want to resize your file. Resize a copy of the document to change the square pixels into rectangular pixels.

❶ Save your file.

❷ Then choose File>Save As and resave another version with a new name.

❸ Go to Image>Image Size.

❹ Make sure Constrain Proportions is not checked.

❺ Change the height from 534 to 480.

❻ Click OK.

❼ Save your new file.

486 Footage

Sometimes we still deal with footage shot on Beta SP or footage that has been onlined at 720x486. If you are ever working with 486 footage:

❶ Import the file into After Effects.

❷ Make a new 720x480 composition.

❸ Drag the footage into the timeline.

❹ Select the layer and move its position one pixel up or down.

You are cropping a couple of lines off the top, and four off the bottom but you won't miss them. You need to move the file by one pixel to preserve the field order.

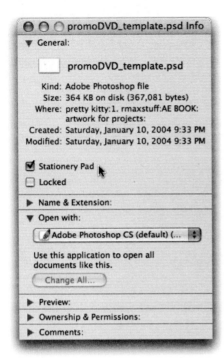

Templates in Photoshop for Macintosh

Do you find that you're modifying the presets in Photoshop? Maybe all the menus in the DVD you're building are a certain color background, or you have the same heading on numerous slideshow files? If so, consider using a template. The best way to do this on a Mac is as a Stationery Pad:

❶ Create a file with the specifications you need.

❷ Save it to your project file.

❸ Navigate to the file in the finder.

❹ Go to File>Get Info or select the file and press Cmd+I.

❺ Click the Stationery Pad box.

❻ Close the Get Info window.

When you open a stationery file, an untitled copy of the original is opened. To make any changes to this file, uncheck the Stationery box, modify then save the file again. Remember to check the stationery box again.

The process is not quite as elegant on a Windows machine. You can make the file read only by right-clicking on a file's icon and choosing properties. This will force you to choose Save As, hence preserving the original document.

Color Safe

If you're animating for output directly onto DVD, you don't necessarily have to worry about using true broadcast safe colors. Some TVs are oversaturated, however, so it's not a bad idea to apply the Broadcast Colors Effect.

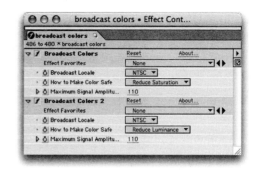

❶ In a 720x480 composition, press the Home key to go back to the beginning the composition.

❷ Choose Layer>New>Adjustment Layer.

❸ Choose Effect>Video>Broadcast Colors.

❹ Choose NTSC or PAL and choose Reduce Saturation. The default maximum signal level of 110 is good.

❺ Render your Movie.

You can also apply a second Broadcast Colors Effect to reduce Luminance as well as Saturation. Under no case should you use Photoshop's NTSC Colors filter because it is inferior.

Button... Button

If you're using AE 6.5 and Adobe Encore... you are in luck. After Effects can automate the button and overlay creating process for you.

❶ In the Timeline select all the layers that make up the button

❷ Choose Layer>Adobe Encore DVD>Create Button and name the button

❸ Use the pop-up boxes to assign highlight layers and a video thumbnail, After Effects will create new compositions and name them properly for Encore.

❹ You then need to open the button composition up.

❺ Make sure all quality switches are set to maximum quality and view the comp at 100% to check for 'weirdness.'

❻ Choose Composition>Save Frame As>Photoshop Layers. Be sure to retain the (+) prefix so Encore will read the file as a button.

Splash Screen to Still Menu

Do you want an initial animation to introduce your DVD? This is known as a Splash screen and usually transitions to the main menu. To do this you need to have a track as the first play item that jumps to the main menu.

① Design a 720x480 menu in Photoshop. Make sure you don't have any active layer styles, blending modes, or adjustment layers. If you do, flatten and merge the layers. Also, make sure you are not using color management.

② Import the file as a composition into After Effects.

③ Import any audio into the composition.

④ Make position keyframes for your buttons and place them at the end of your animation. Your buttons should end up in the exact position you imported them.

⑤ Animate your elements, and output your file with the Animation Codec (uncompressed audio if you are using audio).

⑥ MPEG-2 encode your track.

⑦ Import your menu and animated MPEG track into your DVD authoring program.

⑧ Select the track as the first play item.

⑨ Select the track and make the Main Menu the End Jump item.

There might be a short delay when you preview this transition in your DVD authoring application. The best way to check if this is working is to format your DVD and create an Audio_TS and Video_TS file. Open your DVD player and play the Video_TS file.

Splash Screen to Still Menu II

Did you know you can create a Photoshop layered menu file without ever opening Photoshop? After Effects is a strong design tool as well as an animation application. You can create your elements in AE, and export an animated splash track and a layered Photoshop file.

❶   Create a new 720x480 comp in AE.

❷   Create new solid layers and apply effects.

❸   To use circular buttons, choose Effect>Render>Circle.

❹   To use square buttons, make your solids 100x100 and scale down to the appropriate size.

❺   Name your layers, and make sure your normal button states are the bottommost layers in the timeline, with selected above them and activated states above all other states.

❻   Type your text. If your text will be over a button state, make sure the text is above all the states in the timeline.

❼   Animate your elements and export the animation.

❽   Go to the last frame of your animation, and choose Composition>Save Frame as>Photoshop Layers.

❾   In your DVD authoring application, set up the track as the first play item and make it jump to the layered menu when finished.

Looping (Not)

No matter how carefully you prepare a loop in After Effects, there will be a delay when you watch the authored DVD. Why? Because the players have to jump the laser back. Depending upon the quality of the DVD player, that could mean a minor delay or forever.

❶   Create a single looping Background in AE.

❷   Render the file and re-import it back into your AE project.

❸   In the Project window, press Cmd+F (Ctrl+F) to tell the menu to loop 3–6 times.

❹   Add the file into a comp by dragging it on the new comp icon. The duration and dimensions will be set automatically.

         •   Add music to your menu.

❺   Re-render the file (with Sound) and then MPEG-2 encode the file.

This way, the menu will loop seamlessly a few times (before the 'big jump'). If your viewer can't make their mind up in two minutes, they deserve a 'little' jolt.

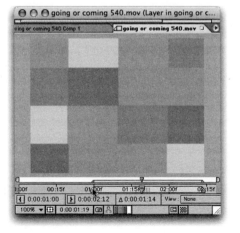

Quick Edits In the Layer Window

•   Select the footage layer in the timeline window and double-click to open it in its layer window. You can make in- and out-points by dragging the triangles on either side of the colored bar, or by pressing the In and Out icons.

•   You can slip the edit by dragging the colored bar left or right.

•   Making new in- and out-points for a layer in the layer window only slips the edit. If you want to change the in-point of the layer in relation to the composition, do so in the timeline window.

Quick Edits In the Timeline

To trim a layer in the timeline, drag the triangles on either end of the clip to a new point in time.

If you are at a frame when you want an edit to begin, press Option+[(that's left bracket) (Alt+[ ) to trim the beginning of the layer or Option+] (that's right bracket) (Alt+]) to trim the end of the layer.

Once you have in and out points, you can slip your edit in the timeline using the Pan Behind Tool.

Tool.

❶   Select the layer

❷   Choose the Pan Behind Tool

❸   Mouse over the layer in the timeline and drag either left or right to slip the edit.

To trim numerically, expand the In and Out Columns and enter your desired In- and Out-points. Changing Duration will stretch the layer.

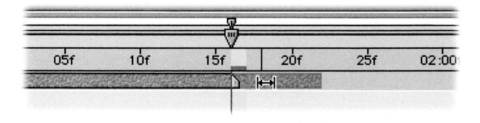

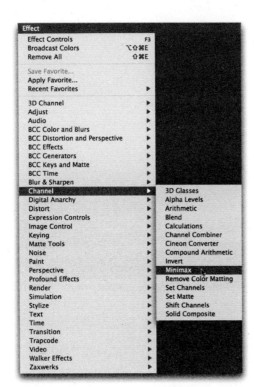

Quick Motion Background I

Need to make something in a hurry? You can make great looking motion backgrounds quickly using Illustrator and simple, fast effects in AE. Subtlety is the key.

❶ Open Illustrator and create a new 720x534 file. Illustrator does not support Pixel Aspect Ratio Correction.

❷ Select the Rectangle Tool or press M on your

❸ Draw a rectangle with a fill but no stroke.

❹ Duplicate the rectangle and fill the art board with rectangles.

❺ Change the color of the rectangles so that no two colors are next to each other. Do this by selecting a shape and clicking on a color in the swatches palette.

❻ Select every second row of rectangles by Shift Clicking on shapes, and drag the bounding box to the left and right to elongate the selected rectangles.

❼ With the rectangles still selected, choose Object>Arrange>Send to Back.

❽ Save the file, and Import it into AE flattened as footage.

❾ Drag the file to the New Composition button in the Project Window.

❿ Select the layer and choose Effect>Channel>Minimax.

⓫ In the Effects Palette Choose: Operation Maximum, Channel>Color, Direction>Horizontal & Vertical.

⓬ Animate the Radius of this effect until satisfied.

⓭ You might also want to add an adjustment layer and try adding Boris Tritone, Colorama or Turbulent Displace.

⓮ When you are finished, choose Composition>Composition Settings and change the ratio to 720x480.

Back in the timeline, select the 720x534 layer, and press Cmd+Option+F (Ctrl+Alt+F) to scale to fit the layer.

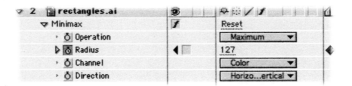

Quick Motion Background II

Add a bit of subtle action. Using the same file you created in the last tip, here's how.

❶ In After Effects go to File>Import>Footage and select the rectangle file.

❷ Drag the file to the New Composition button in the Project Window.

❸ Select the layer, and press S to open the scale property.

❹ Make two keyframes: one for 200 percent and a few seconds later for 100 percent.

❺ Duplicate the layer and apply a multiply mode to the top layer.

❻ Select the top layer. Press U to show the Scale keyframes.

❼ Select the keyframes and choose Animation>Keyframe Assistant>Time Reverse Keyframes.

❽ Reduce the opacity of the top layer as desired.

❾ Do a RAM Preview by pressing 0 on the numeric keypad.

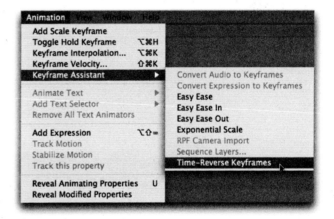

Quick Motion Background III

To begin with, create a seamless pattern in Photoshop. There are several ways to do this.

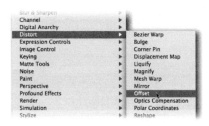

- You can download a seamless pattern, and tile it. Check www.autofx.com for several free textures in their Download Software area.

- Use the Patternmaker command.

- Use Offset and Clone to create a seamless pattern.

- Learn more about these techniques in CMP's *Photoshop for Nonlinear Editors*.

For quick seamless motion of any seamless background try the Offset Effect!

❶ Select a layer, and choose Effect>Distort>Offset.

❷ Animate the Shift Center on the X and/or Y axis.

Rendering

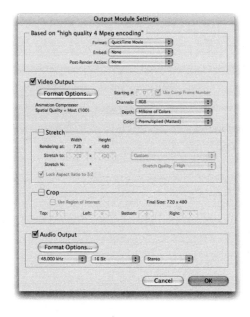

Whether you're coming from Final Cut Pro, Avid, or After Effects, you should output the cleanest file you can. This means applying the least amount of compression. If you are using a Macintosh (or even a Windows machine), it's best to render a QuickTime file.

- Use a lossless codec like Animation.

- Choose the correct field order, and make your audio is 48 kHz. If your audio is 44.1 kHz like that found on audio CDs, export it, as is, because most MPEG encoders will convert the audio to the correct sample rate.

- If you are outputting an animation without progressive video footage (not interlaced), frame render instead of field rendering.

- Make a Render Template for uncompressed output and call it DVD Settings so you will render your DVD files consistently. See Chapter 15 for more on how to create Render Templates.

MPEG 2 Encoding

MPEG 2 encode your tracks before you import them into a DVD authoring program. Some programs allow you to import files that haven't been MPEG-encoded. These give you the option of MPEG encoding in the background or when you format the project.

Background encoding can slow down your computer when you are designing the DVD. Opting to encode on building makes calculating the available run time for the disc difficult. You also won''t get an accurate representation of how much space is being used on the disc.

- For the highest quality results with MPEG 2 encoders, pick the slowest encoding preset.

- Use two pass variable bitrate encoding if possible. Set the lowest bitrate to 4 and the highest bitrate at or below 7.5. Otherwise the disc may skip on some set-top boxes (and most computers).

- It's a good idea to AAC encode all you audio even if your DVD authoring program can use AIFF files. Make sure the audio files are the same length as the video files.

- Save all DVD ready files to a DVD ready folder within your project folder.

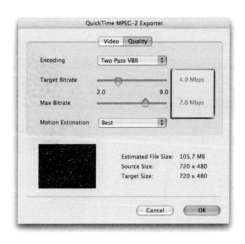

Don't Rush to Encode

We know Adobe is trying to improve workflow by including the Main Concept MPEG2 encoder in AE 6.5 for Windows. In theory it sounds like a great idea to go directly to MPEG 2... but don't rush. In order to get the highest quality and smallest size, you need to perform a two pass Variable Bit Rate encoding (VBR). This approach works by analyzing a file and then compressing it. So unless your copy of After Effects is clairvoyant, you can't analyze a file before it's rendered. Always go to the Animation codec, and THEN convert to MPEG 2. Remember, slow and steady wins the race (at least it always worked for the turtle on TV).

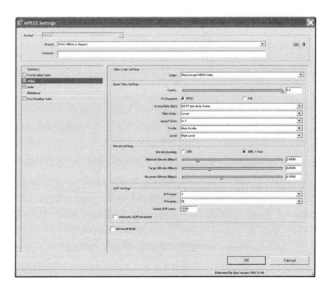

ON THE SPOT

How to Beat the Render Queue:
Advanced Render Strategies to Save Time

Welcome to the finish line… or the end of the road. This is where your good ideas and hard work bear results. Inside the Render Queue is where your motion graphics come to life. But birth can be painful, or easy, it all depends on your approach.

This chapter will share several secrets to gain back time and achieve consistent results with your render. By harnessing templates and After Effects' powerful media management abilities, your graphics will come to live faster (and with fewer errors). Stop wasting time and get the results you need, faster!

Quick Path to Consistency

You've gone through all the trouble to set up your render and tweak your render and output settings. Now save those custom settings for future use.

❶ Click on the render settings or Output Module pop-up menu.

❷ Choose Make Template from the list.

Be Consistent

Want consistent results? Use templates. After Effects comes with several built-in templates that addresses several of the more common production needs. After Effects offers both render setting templates (for establishing quality, resolution, and duration) and output module (for defining file formats). If these built-in options don't do it for you however, you can easily create your own.

❶ Choose Edit > Templates> Render Settings… or Output Module….

❷ Click New to create a new setting or Duplicate to modify a copy of an existing setting.

❸ Modify the settings to match your needs. When finished click OK.

❹ If you'd like, you can choose one of your settings to be the default.

Changing Standards

Want to define the default standards for your render settings out Output module? Sure you could go all the way up to the Edit menu, but why bother when you can set it in the render queue.

❶ Be sure your current setting of choice is saved as a template.

❷ Hold down the Command (Control) key as you select the preset name.

❸ The default settings are now changed for all future comps added to the render queue.

Free Your RAM

Want to give AE more power to devote solely to your render? Try these tips to dedicate your computer's power.

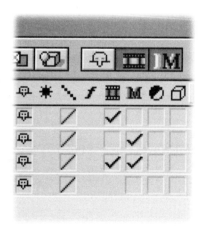

- Choose Edit > Purge > All to release any RAM being held by previews or cache files

- Close the Comp Window (unless you like watching paint dry). This will free up more memory and computer resources for the render. The more layers you have, the bigger benefit in closing this window.

- Quit any other applications running.

- Leave After Effects as the foreground application (in other words if you need to check email or play solitaire, use another machine).

Blurring and Blending Time

Many people are attracted to Frame Blending and Motion Blur. While its true that these settings can generate smoother motion quality, they only do so in specific situations.

- Enable motion blur on a layer if you are animating its position, rotation, scale, or anchor point greatly. This will add realistic blur as the object changes speed. Applying motion blur to slow moving, or static objects has no visible effect (except on your render times). Also, motion blur has no impact for most effects if the motion is created within an effect (such as the Offset or Basic 3D effect). Notably, the Particle Playground effect however is affected by Motion Blur.

- Enable frame blending only if you have changed the speed of a clip. It is most helpful on clips that have been slowed down. However there are some benefits on sped up clips as well. The point here is that frame blending is useless unless there is a speed change in the clip.

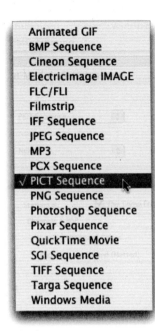

Rendering Stills Instead of Movies

Instead of rendering to QuickTime or AVI, you might consider going to an image sequence. After Effects allows you to write your render to s series of consecutive PICT, PNG, TARGA, or TIFF files. The benefits of this method include.

- You can use QuickTime to spot-check the render partway, without interrupting the render. Thus if the thing doesn't look how you want, you don't have to wait till the entire render is finished to find that out.

- Crashes, power outages, etc. don't hurt so badly, because you just pick up where you left off.

- Nearly all video and 3D applications can import an image sequence; hence you can get around the issue of codecs and such.

  You can specify which can of image sequence you'd like in an output module. Just be sure to create a new folder to hold the rendered frames, otherwise your desktop or drive will get pretty cluttered.

Tip idea by Mark Simpson, Jam Digital, Redondo Beach, California, USA

Render Once, Output Many

A common misunderstanding about rendering is that many think you must render for each output that you want. In other words if you need a movie at different compressions and want an image sequence, you must render each separately, Fortunately, this is FAR from true.

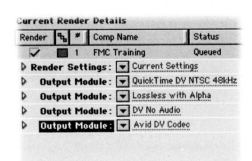

❶ Highlight the required sequence in the Render Queue.

❷ Choose Composition > Add Output Module.

❸ Modify the settings to suit your needs.

❹ Save the project.

❺ Click Render when you are ready to launch the Render Queue.

When the Render Files Are Flowing

There's nothing worse than running out of space in the middle of a batch render. You return expecting everything to be done; yet you are confronted with warnings that rendering was aborted due to a lack of space. If you have additional internal or external drives, a quick change to your preferences may eliminate the problem.

❶ You need to access your preferences menu. Choose After Effects > Preferences > Output (Edit > Preferences > Output).

❷ In the Overflow volumes area you can specify up to 5 drives to handle renders when the original volume fills up.

❸ While you are there, be sure that the Minimum Disk Space Before Overflowing box is set to at least 500 MB. Otherwise you may experience data loss or hard rive lock-up.

❹ Click OK.

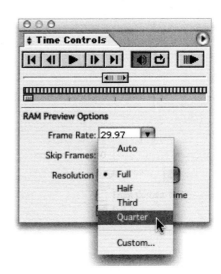

Getting the Most From Your Machine

We are firm believers that old computers should not be sold, but rather re-purposed. It is not uncommon for a professional motion graphic artist to tie up 2 to 4 machines with their workflow. Here are some tips for multi-machine environments.

● Learn to preview your compositions at reduced quality. In other words, set the comp window to Full or Half Quality (depending on your comfort level), but perform RAM previews at Quarter Quality.

● Increase the RAM in your older machines until they are maxed out. AE eats RAM like potato chips.

● Build on all machines, but use your best machine as the render horse. While an iMac or old laptop may be great for building your animations, you'd be MUCH better off sending it over to a dual Xeon (or better yet a G5) to chew through that render.

Render SD and DV Simultaneously

Are you producing animations for multiple formats? Chances are likely that you'll often need both a DV and a Standard Definition output. Simple enough right? Render twice... if you like wasting time that is. A better way is to use two output modules.

1. Set your initial composition up at the larger size, such as 720 X 486.

2. Add the comp to the render queue and set the Render Settings. For best results choose to Field Render with lower field first.

3. Next, set your output module for the first video and choose the settings you need.

4. For the Digital Video render, add a second output module by choosing Composition> Add Output Module.

5. Set this new output module for DV by choosing the QuickTime DV NTSC 48kHz setting.

6. In the second output module, the one for DV, we need to remove six lines of information. It is important to preserve field order. Click on the Output Module name to open its settings.

7. Check the Crop box and specify to crop 2 lines from the top and 4 from the bottom.

8. Name both output modules, be sure to clearly identify the DV render with a unique name.

9. Close all open windows except for the render queue.

10. Save your work.

11. Click Render

Kick it to the Queue

Ready to add a comp to your render queue? Simply press Command + Shift + / (control + Shift + /). To send it on its way. An easy way to think of this shortcuts it to look at the keys involved, Shift plus / generates a question mark. So you can think of this tip as Command + QUEstion... pretty close to Queue.

A Smaller Render

Do you need to limit your render size so it can fit on a particular type of media? Say 640 MB so you can burn them to CD-R for delivery to your client? You can configure After Effects so movies automatically segment at a certain file size.

❶   You need to access your preferences menu. Choose After Effects > Preferences > Output (Edit > Preferences > Output).

❷   Check the Segment Movie Files At box and specify the desired size. For example use 640 MB for a standard CD-ROM and 4.3 GB for a DVD-ROM.

❸   Click OK.

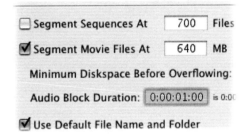

Need to Render Both Field Orders?

Need to render an animation for multiple video systems? Perhaps you need to create a video file for use on older ABVB Avid systems (upper field first) and newer Meridien-based systems (lower field first). Field rendering is set in the Render Settings, not the Output module.

Solution #1: Render twice.

Solution #2: Add a second Output Module. For the upper field first movie, enter +1 in the Top field and –1 in the Bottom field.

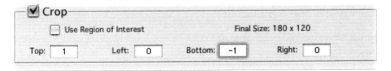

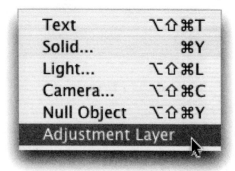

The Power to Adjust

Instead of running a blur or levels command on each layer of your composition, try applying it to all layers simultaneously. One effect can often render faster than 5 effects. The Adjustment layers work very well for global adjustments.

❶ Choose Layer > New > Adjustment Layer.

❷ Apply any needed filter to the Adjustment Layer

❸ All layers below will be affected.

❹ To modify the strength of the adjustment, you can change the Adjustment Layer's opacity and blend mode.

Get it Together

Oftentimes in the middle of a creative session, we get a little sloppy. We find ourselves dragging files in, dumping things on the desktop, or even reading right from a network. That's fine when you are sitting in front of the machine, but we prefer our renders to be autonomous. The best way to ensure a smooth render is to pull all files together into one folder.

❶ Choose File > Collect Files

❷ Specify if you want files For All Comps, For Selected Comps, or only for Queued Comps.

❸ When ready, click Collect.

❹ The needed files will be copied to a new folder that you specify. The original files are still left behind.

❺ You can choose to leave the original files around (in case other projects or users need them) or manually erase them.

❻ To find stray files, you can also run the Collect Files Feature on the original project, but this time generate a report only.

Where Do You Work?

Setting the Work Area is very important. It allows you to define what portion of your composition is loaded for RAM previews as well as define which portion to render. You can set the Work Area by dragging handles in the Timeline Window, however there is a more precise method.

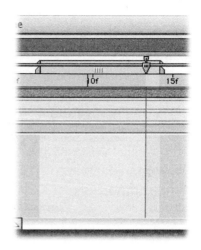

1 Position your Current Time Indicator at the beginning of the Work Area and press B (for Beginning).

2 Position your Current Time Indicator at the end of the Work Area and press N (for eNd).

Alternately, you can use your selected layers to define the Work Area. Simply press Cmd + Option + B (Ctrl + Alt + B) to set the Work Area to selection.

The BIG Weekend Render

If we have several projects that we need to output, we'll often create a 'rendering' project. This way we can set up one render queue and really leave our machines unattended for a while.

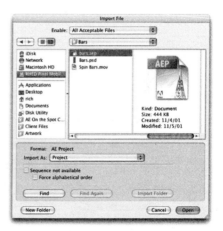

1 Set up the individual projects as needed, including adding items to the render queue and specifying settings

2 Create a new project and save it.

3 Choose File > Import > File or press Cmd+I (Ctrl+I).

4 Select the projects you'd like to import and merge together.

5 Check the Render Queue and make sure all of the output paths are still valid.

6 Save the Project.

7 Click Render and go enjoy the weekend or a night away from the office for a while.

Choose File...

email_methods.jsx
email_setup.jsx
newRenderLocations.jsx
render_and_email.jsx
renderNamedItems.jsx
save_and_increment.jsx
smartImport.jsx

The Most Important Email All Week

After Effects 6 now supports scripts. One of those scripts can actually render a file then email you upon completion. If you're a tech geek, the gears in your head are already spinning. Most pagers and cell phones can receive text messages via the Internet. Just think, the leash has been cut!

❶ Open up your General Preferences and be sure that the Allow Scripts to Write Files and Access Network box is checked.

❷ Add your files to the Render Queue like normal.

❸ Choose File > Run Script > render_and_email.jsx, you will now be prompted for your email settings.

❹ Enter server smtp address: such as mail.mac.com, click OK

❺ Enter the reply to address: such as the email you want to use to send the message.

❻ If your server required log-in (most do), click YES and enter your ID and password. Click OK.

❼ Enter the recipients email address. Click OK

❽ An email with the subject AE Render complete will be sent when the queue is finished.

How cool is that?

Need a Low Quality Render to Email?

You are happy with your animation and have successfully previewed it using RAM Preview. Now its time to send it over to the client or producer for approval. Time to go to the render queue right? Not so fast... you just rendered it. Save some time.

- You can create and save a RAM Preview simultaneously by pressing Cmd + 0 on the numeric keypad (Ctrl + 0 on numeric keypad).

- You can create and save a Shift RAM Preview simultaneously by pressing Cmd + Shift + 0 on the numeric keypad (Ctrl + Shift + 0 on numeric keypad).

Saving Render Time at the Other End

After effects creates graphics using the full RGB spectrum of values. This can cause problems when they are brought into nonlinear editing systems. Some systems such as those made by Avid as you if you used RGB values when you import, this will properly compensate for the difference between RGB and YUV color spaces. Most systems however will not make this fix, so you can save render time on the Nonlinear Editing side by getting your color right in AE.

❶ Create a new adjustment layer at the top of your layer stack by choosing Layer > New > Adjustment Layer.

❷ Apply the Broadcast Safe Effect (Effect > Video > Broadcast Safe).

❸ Specify your format of choice (NTSC or PAL) in the Broadcast Locale menu.

❹ Adjust the Maximum Signal sliders to set the IRE level at which pixels above will be altered. The range is between 100 to 120 IRE. A level of 100 can cause noticeable color shift while a level of 120 is often considered risky. The default value of 110 IRE units is usually the best choice.

Broadcast Colors
Reduce Interlace Flicker
Timecode

Mobile Workflow

Once you get into things, you may want to be mobile. Keep your media in one folder on a portable drive. Here's a real-world situation and advice from an experienced After Effect artist.

"If I have ten section titles all based on the same basic layout, I will build the first four," said Rich Rubasch of Tilt Media. He then copies the project to another machine and starts it rendering. Then he returns to the original computer and "finishes the builds on the first system.)

By remembering to use multiple machines, an AE artist can speed up their render workflow.

RHED Pixel Mobile 3

281

Got Transparency?

Need to render your file so you can composite it in another application such as an editing application? Be sure to choose a codec (compressor decompressor) that supports embedded alpha channels. Many users will prefer the animation codec as it provides a good balance of quality to size.

❶ Click on the Output Module in the Render Queue

❷ Choose Animation codec by clicking on the Format Options button and selecting it from the next window.

❸ While there specify Millions + colors. Click OK.

❹ The Channels menu should now say RGB + ALPHA and depth set to Millions of Colors +. If not, adjust them so they are properly set.

❺ Your animation is likely pre-multiplied against Black so change it to set the color to Straight (Unmatted).

❻ Click OK and Render when ready.

Need to Re-render?

For one reason or another, it always happens, the need to rerender. Perhaps a small tweak to a keyframe or a timing issue. Chances are while your animation may have needed refining, the render queue was perfect. Save yourself some time and Re-Queue that animation.

❶ Select a previously rendered animation.

❷ Press Command + Shift + D (Control + Shift + D) to duplicate the render item with the same settings and output name. This will rewrite over the previous file to the exact same destination.

❸ Save your work, then click Render when ready to output.

More RAM Previews

By now you've probably noticed that the importance of RAM previews. There is the standard one which you normally see in the Time Control Window and can be invoked by pressing 0 on the numeric keypad.

The other RAM Preview controls can be accessed by click on the words "RAM Preview Options." This preview is usually a lower quality method, but can be configured to the user's preference. To launch this alternate preview, Shift + click on the Preview button or press Shift + 0 on the numeric keypad.

Lossless Codecs

Want to speed up your render times? Try pre-rendering backgrounds and other elements in a complex composition? You can of course turn to the Lossless Animation codec, but better options exist.

Theory, LLC offers two products that do the trick well.

- QuickTime NONE16 codec is freeware. The obvious benefit is cost, but you do not get the benefits of support. The file produces excellent quality when rendering out 16 bit files.

- If you want to move up a level, check out the affordable Microcosm codec. Microcosm is the world's first lossless 64bit QuickTime codec for creating 64-bit or 32-bit files at a fraction of their original size.

For more information on both Microcosm and NONE16, check out www.digitalanarchy.com.

In the Neighborhood

Part of render speed is determined by how quickly your source files can be accessed. Trying to read media files from a network or an optical drive can significantly impact render times. For best results, copy all source files to the local machine. You should always try to run media from internal drives or s high-speed disk array.

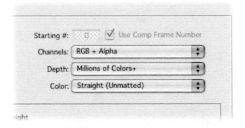

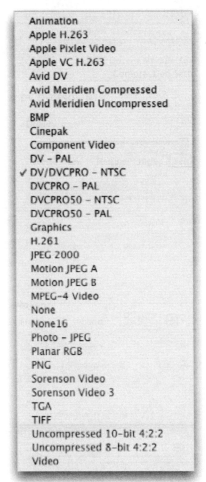

Keyable Movies

Want to create a QuickTime Movie that can be keyed through an alpha channel? It's very do-able if you know what options to pick.

❶ Determine if your codec supports embedded alpha channels. Many uncompressed or low compression formats do. If you are using DV however, you must choose Animation.

❷ Be sure to choose RGB + Alpha in the Output dialog box if it is an option.

❸ Specify Millions of Colors + if you want to embed an alpha as well.

Render out your file or Export. As long as you have chosen a proper codec and specified to include the alpha, you will get great results when keying your graphic.

Kooky Codecs

A Codec is a Compressor/Decompressor that allows you to write an animation file to a smaller size that can then be read (without conversion) into a nonlinear editing system. Many designers are confused about WHAT codec to use when rendering from their AE timeline. There are several things to consider when outputting your file.

● Always check with the editor or producer who is going to be using the file to find out specifics about the edit system to be used.. Be sure to get version numbers as codecs will often change depending upon which version of the editing software is in place.

● Most NLE manufacturers post codecs and render specs on their websites. Look in their support or download section for details,

● A detailed and helpful website for information about using After Effects and Avid Editing systems is www.wesplate.com. Wes is the creator of Automatic Duck (www.automaticduck.com), a helpful utility for moving Avid and Final Cut Pro timelines into After Effects.

● When in doubt, use the Lossless setting. This will use the Animation codec, an incredibly high-quality codec that is universal. File sizes will be larger (and you will have to convert upon import or in the timeline) but they file is 'universal.'

The "Other" Render Queue

After Effects can output several specialized formats, however you won't find them in the render queue. Instead, check File>Export for several specialized formats. Some options (like the FLV exporter) require you to have optional software installed. Here's a list of some that you may encounter:

Adobe Motion Exchange (.amx) for LM2	Allows you to save data out for use in a LiveMotion project. LiveMotion is SWF authoring tool from Adobe that supports advanced animation.
Macromedia Flash (SWF)	This will write a standard Macromedia SWF file in the Flash 5 format.
AIFF	An audio only format used mostly by Macintosh machines
AVI	A 'well established' windows video format
DV Stream	A raw stream of Digital Video.
Image Sequence	A series of still graphics for each frame of the comp. Useful for sending files when the output codec is questionable.
Macromedia Flash Video (FLV)	If you have Flash MX 2004 Professional installed, you can write a compressed video format that works well for Flash authoring.
MPEG-4	A compressed file format for web delivery. It is usually better to render a QuickTime first, then compress
QuickTime Movie	Use the Render Queue instead
Wave	An audio only format used mostly by Windows machines
μ Law	An audio only format

Where Did You Go?

Need to find a file after you rendered it? No problem, just flip the triangle down next to Output Module in the Render Queue. For all completed renders, you should see a drive name and the file listed. Click on the blue link and it will reveal the file for you at the Finder (desktop) level.

285

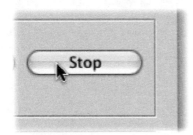

A Better Stop

Normally when you click Stop on an item in the render queue, it adds it to the bottom of the list and will pick up where it left off. That may be what you want, but often you intended to bust the render, tweak it, and re-render. To stop a render and re-queue it to begin at the beginning, hold down the Option (Alt) key when clicking Stop Render. This will avoid the pickup and add the item to be re-rendered from the start of the original output settings.

After Thoughts

After Effects offers you a powerful feature called Post-Render Actions. These allow you to choose from a list of pre-defined actions that you'd like to happen after the file is rendered.

❶   Choose Composition>Pre-render or flip down the triangle next to the Output Module of an existing item in the render queue.

❷   Choose one of the following Post-Render Actions

- None – Does Nothing (the default)

- Import – Adds the rendered file into the project window when rendering is complete

- Import & Replace Usage – Imports the file into the project and replaces usage for specified items. You determine which files will be replaced via the pickwhip. We find this most useful to replace precompositions that appear in multiple comps (such as the motion background in a group of show bumpers).

- Set Proxy – Allows you to use the rendered file as a proxy for a specified project item (again use the pickwhip). This will speed up previews. For more on proxies, be sure to look at Chapter 11.

The X-Factor

by Bill Love

After Effects 6.5 Pro adds some REALLY cool software as far as networked rendering goes. We've only just begun to play with the new X-Factor developed by GridIron Software. But its results are impressive. It allows you to gang up to 3 machines together to tackle a tough render. It even allows you to gang machines up for preview purposes.

Few things to keep in mind:

- We've seen results nearly three-times faster by using three comparable machines.

- The software is well documented and easy to set-up. It uses a peer-to-peer approach with no administration, configuration, or management needed,

- You can buy more licenses if you want to go beyond the three machine limit.

- On a Mac, you must install XLR8 must be installon the same hard drive as After Effects.

- Don't have footage items with the same filename. Even if they reside in different directories, it wil cause problems when rendering.

- You can even take a few older machines and add to your render station. Just get the machines configured and then leave them waiting to help.

- You'll get better results using Ethernet networks rather than wireless, but both work.

- Be sure to check out Adobe's help documentation as well as GridIron Software for more information (www.gridironsoftware.com).

Acknowledgments

My wife, Meghan, for her patience, love, and commitment. As we welcome our first child into the world, I am grateful you are by my side.

My family for their support and guidance. All that I have, I owe to you. Thanks for all of the good advice and teaching throughout the years.

My coauthors, Marcus and Rachel. Thanks for saying "yes" to this idea. Your insight and knowledge have made this a much better book.

–Richard Harrington

Thanks to the strong and supportive AE community, especially Trish and Chris Meyer. Thanks Rich and Marcus for having me be part of this book. And thanks to my friends and family.

–Rachel Max

My best friend and wife, Lisa, who suffers through all my geeky pursuits with grace, humor and intelligence.

My parents, who gave me these After-Effects-loving genes, and who raised me in a house so full of wonders that my mind was continually open. To my brother Daniel, for "sound" advice and long, patient, very helpful emails.

To Rich and Rachel, for sharing my obsession.

–Marcus Geduld

The authors would like to thank the following for making this book possible:

George Annab	DVPA	Mac Design Magazine
Frank Brogan	Dan Ebberts	Trish & Chris Meyer
Kay Christy	The Foundry	NAPP
Dorothy Cox	Future Media Concepts	Jason Paruta
The Creative Cow community	Rod Harlan	Paul Temme
Zax Dow	Scott Kelby	Total Training
DV Magazine	Ben Kozuch	Jim Tierney

THE AUTHORITY ON DIGITAL VIDEO TECHNOLOGY

INSPIRING AND EMPOWERING CREATIVITY

DV
MAGAZINE

DV ·
EXPO AND
CONFERENCES

DV
QUARTERLY

DV
QUARTERLY

DV
.COM

DV
FILM FESTIVAL

DV
EXPERT SERIES
(A DIVISION
OF CMP BOOKS)

FOR PRODUCT DETAILS, GO TO **WWW.DV.COM**

Creating Motion Graphics with After Effects
Volume 1: The Essentials, 3rd Edition

Trish Meyer & Chris Meyer

Master the core concepts and tools you need to tackle virtually every job, including keyframe animation, masking, mattes, and plug-in effects. New chapters demystify Parenting, 3D Space, and features of the latest software version.

$59.95, 4-color, Trade Paper with CD-ROM, 448 pp, ISBN 1-57820-249-3

Photoshop CS for Nonlinear Editors

2nd Edition

Richard Harrington

Use Photoshop CS to generate characters, correct colors, and animate graphics for digital video. You'll grasp the fundamental concepts and master the complete range of Photoshop tools through lively discourse, full-color presentations, and hands-on tutorials. The companion DVD contains 90 minutes of video lessons, tutorial media, and plug-ins.

$54.95, 4-color, Trade Paper with DVD, 336 pp, ISBN 1-57820-237-X

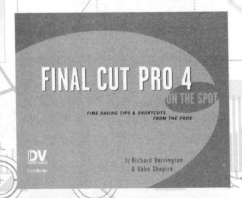

Final Cut Pro 4 On the Spot

Richard Harrington & Abba Shapiro

Packed with more than 350 expert techniques, this book clearly illustrates all the essential methods that pros use to get the job done with Final Cut Pro. Experienced editors and novices alike discover an invaluable reference filled with ways to improve efficiency and creativity.

$27.95, Trade Paper, 236 pp, ISBN 1-57820-231-0

à Jules et Tom

Florence Seyvos – Anaïs Vaugelade

L'ami du petit tyrannosaure

l'école des loisirs
11, rue de Sèvres, Paris 6ᵉ

Il était une fois un petit tyrannosaure qui n'avait pas d'amis parce qu'il les avait tous mangés.

Pourtant, chaque fois, il avait essayé de se retenir très fort. Ça se passait toujours de la même façon.
Le petit tyrannosaure rencontrait quelqu'un qu'il trouvait sympathique et s'asseyait à côté de lui pour engager la conversation.

Au bout de quelques instants, il sentait une petite faim lui chatouiller l'estomac. Alors il regardait discrètement à droite et à gauche pour voir s'il n'y avait pas une ou deux fourmis à grignoter.

Très vite, il se mettait à avoir très faim. Mais comme il trouvait son nouvel ami vraiment très sympathique, il lui proposait d'aller jouer chez lui ou sur la plage.

t c'est là que la catastrophe se produisait.
e petit tyrannosaure se jetait sur son nouvel ami
t n'en faisait qu'une bouchée.

« Pardon ! Pardon ! » disait ensuite le petit tyrannosaure.
Mais bien sûr, c'était trop tard.

Ce matin-là, le petit tyrannosaure venait juste d'avaler son dernier nouvel ami.

Il était seul, à présent. Totalement seul dans la grande forêt.

Il comprit qu'il n'aurait sans doute plus jamais d'ami.

Alors il fut pris d'une immense tristesse et se mit à pleurer.

Il comprit aussi que, bientôt, il allait avoir très faim, et se mit à pleurer encore plus fort.

Quelqu'un s'approcha.

C'était une souris qui s'appelait Mollo et qui venait d'une autre forêt.

« Va-t'en ! » lui cria le petit tyrannosaure. « Va-t'en, sinon je vais te manger ! »
Mollo ne bougea pas.
« Ne t'en fais pas », dit-il, « j'ai le pouvoir de me rendre immangeable.
Il suffit que je prononce une formule dans ma tête et, aussitôt, ça me donne un goût épouvantable. »

«Et là, tu l'as prononcée, cette formule?» demanda le petit tyrannosaure.
«Je viens de le faire», répondit Mollo.
Rassuré, le petit tyrannosaure lui raconta toute son histoire.

«Écoute», lui dit Mollo, «j'ai très envie d'être ton ami. Je suis sûr que c'est possible.

Mais d'abord, il faut que tu manges. Je vais te faire un gâteau. Je suis un excellent pâtissier.»

Tout en répétant sa formule, Mollo ouvrit sa valise-cuisine et fit très vite un bon gros gâteau.

Il s'en coupa un petit morceau et offrit le reste au petit tyrannosaure.

«Tu vois», dit-il, «tu n'as pas tenté de me manger pendant que je préparais le gâteau.

Demain nous essaierons quelque chose de plus difficile et je te promets que, dans trois jours, nous serons amis pour la vie.»

Ensuite ce fut l'heure de dormir et ils se dirent au revoir.

Mollo passa la nuit dans une cachette car il ne savait pas dire sa formule en dormant.

Le lendemain matin, Mollo prépara un gâteau et le mit à cuire. Puis il dit : « Il faut que tu t'entraînes à ne pas me manger. Tu vois, là, par exemple, je n'ai pas dit ma formule. »

Le petit tyrannosaure regarda le gâteau et trouva qu'il mettait beaucoup trop de temps à cuire.

Il se jeta sur Mollo et l'avala tout rond.

Mais le recracha aussitôt, parce qu'il avait vraiment un goût épouvantable.

«Ouf!» dit Mollo, «j'ai tout juste eu le temps de dire ma formule. Nous avons eu chaud.»
Le petit tyrannosaure était bien content que la formule ait marché.
Mais il avait tout de même honte de ce qu'il avait fait, et se sentait très malheureux.
«Ne t'inquiète pas», lui dit Mollo.
«J'ai confiance. Tu vas faire des progrès. Et dans deux jours, nous serons amis pour la vie.»

Comme ils se disaient au revoir, le petit tyrannosaure demanda à Mollo :
« Pourquoi est-ce que tu ne répètes pas tout le temps ta formule ?
Comme ça, tu serais sûr de ne pas être mangé… »
« Parce que », répondit Mollo, « quand je ne suis pas en danger, je préfère avoir bon goût. »

Le lendemain, Mollo dit au petit tyrannosaure que, cette fois, le gâteau allait mettre un peu plus longtemps à cuire. Il lui dit aussi qu'il n'avait pas l'intention de prononcer sa formule.

Le petit tyrannosaure se jeta sur le sol en pleurant.
« Je veux te manger !
Je veux te manger ! Je veux te manger ! » hurla-t-il.

Mais il ne mangea pas Mollo car le gâteau fut prêt juste à temps.
«Tu verras», lui dit Mollo, «il nous reste encore une toute petite chose à réussir,
et demain, je sens que nous serons amis pour la vie.»

Le lendemain, Mollo avait un drôle d'air et un bras dans le plâtre.
« Je me suis cassé le bras », dit-il. « C'est embêtant, parce que je ne peux pas faire de gâteau. »
« Tu vas avoir faim », ajouta-t-il.
« Très faim.
Mais je ne dirai pas ma formule. Si tu veux, tu peux me manger.
Vas-y. Mange-moi. »

Le petit tyrannosaure répondit :
«Je crois que je vais faire un gâteau. Tu veux bien m'expliquer la recette?»

Et c'est ainsi que le petit tyrannosaure fit le premier gâteau de sa vie…

... et réussit à ne pas manger son ami.

Quand le gâteau fut cuit, Mollo enleva son plâtre.
«Je ne me suis pas cassé le bras en vrai», dit-il. «Tu ne m'en veux pas d'avoir menti?»
Le petit tyrannosaure ne lui en voulait pas du tout. Il était fier, heureux,
et il avait enfin un ami pour la vie.